ENDORSEMENTS

Divorce is an ugly word that encompasses not just the action itself but also the long-lasting, devastating ramifications. There are stigmas—some applied by society, but often self-inflicted—resulting from a marriage breakup. The author of *Rebuild, Restore, Renew*, Gladys Thompson has been there. She's felt the pain and harsh impact of divorce. Her experiences have given her unique insights as she navigated the pain, the loss, and a vastly changed reality.

In *Rebuild, Restore, Renew,* she shares deeply personal lessons presented in a series of practical, motivational daily devotionals. They are aimed mostly at Christians but are useful and powerful sources of comfort and strategies for anyone working through divorce. They can also be used by those who have suffered life-changing rejection or separation through job loss or even death.

These short and powerful devotionals offer comforting words as well as suggested, practical actions and responses. They are a simple step-by-step aid for those coping with the nasty reality of divorce.

The book can be read in small, daily bits as intended. But they can also be consumed in larger chunks at a time. Depending on the reader's needs and emotions, they can be read daily or in haphazard order.

Rebuild, Restore, Renew helps readers journey through the rocky, uncharted, and often unexpected hurdles towards restoration and renewal.

This is a must-read, practical guide for those dealing with divorce. It offers a rope of hope to those just 'clinging on.' Highly recommended.

—**Barrie Doyle**, author of the Oak Grove Conspiracies novels
and *Musick for the King,* www.barriedoyle.com

When Gladys was hit by the trauma of divorce, she decided to respond redemptively. Whether that was a conscious choice or a result of living a life of faith, it was the path she followed. In her devotionals, she shares something of the journey she embarked on at that time.

With wisdom, Gladys chose to look at where she was and determine the direction in which she wished to go as she sorted through the complications that this unexpected and unanticipated disaster brought to her. As she slowly rose to her feet, she chose to engage in the process of rebuilding, restoring and renewing that continues in her life to this day.

Her companion on the journey was the Holy Spirit, and her guidebook was the Bible. As she began to apply the teaching from these sources to her life, she realized they could be useful to others on a similar journey and has offered them in her book. One thing that I appreciate is the way that scriptural ideas are so closely intertwined with everyday living. The practical suggestions offered help in the building of a new life.

I have been spared the pain of divorce, but there are other traumas that I have known, and I found that many of the experiences and helpful lessons that Gladys shares are equally relevant for me. My prayer is that all who read this will come away with renewed hope, greater faith and confidence in God's presence in the midst of our difficult days, as I was.

I commend to you *Rebuild, Restore, Renew: Growing in Christ While Going through Divorce*.

—**Eleanor Shepherd**, award-winning author of
More Questions than Answers: Sharing Faith by Listening

Sometimes our life journey takes us into territory we do not expect and for which we are unprepared. At such times, it is good to have a companion who has travelled similar roads and, although their journey is not identical, has the insight to help us along the way. Gladys is just such a welcome friend. I have known her as a co-worker and friend as she walked her journey of divorce, the loss of her original ministry career, and her devastating car accident. She takes the wisdom of Scripture, reflects on how it has helped her, and, with transparency and a touch of humour, speaks to issues that may be timely as you travel your own journey. And for every day, there is a prayer. It may or may not be the exact prayer that you would pray, but I am confident it will open a line of communication between you and the God who not only walked with Gladys but who also will walk with you.

—**David Freeman**, Associate Pastor, Gateway Church, Caledonia, ON

As a pastor, I have observed that experiencing divorce is not unlike going through the various stages of grief after the death of a spouse. I have often wished that there were more tools available in pastoring such hurting people. Gladys Thompson has now handed us such a tool. Gladys is not naïve enough to suggest that healing will happen overnight, but these devotionals are designed to bring us back from the edges of hope to a more deeply formed and focused faith that motivates us to rebuild our broken world with confidence and resilience. I believe God will greatly use these devotionals to help many people who are facing life after divorce and others who will read these to assist them with other forms of difficulty.

—**Colonel Lindsay Rowe**, Retired Salvation Army Officer

In *Rebuild, Restore, Renew*, Gladys recounts the two "divorces" that she faced with a candour that expresses the depth of pain and loss that crushed her dreams and changed the course of her life. As her story is revealed, each chapter tells not just the painful experiences but also the lessons and workings of God along the way as He rebuilt and restored her life to one of purpose and renewed joy.

Life isn't always fair, but God promises His presence and guidance to those who seek to rebuild their lives based on the foundational principles of His Word. This book is for anyone seeking hope and wondering if life after divorce or loss is possible.

—**Bev Broughton**, chaplain and former facilitator of
Divorce Recovery support groups

REBUILD,
RESTORE,
RENEW

REBUILD, RESTORE, RENEW

Growing in Christ While
Going through Divorce

GLADYS THOMPSON

Printed in Canada

ISBN: 978-1-4866-2167-5
eBook ISBN: 978-1-4866-2168-2

Word Alive Press
119 De Baets Street Winnipeg, MB R2J 3R9
www.wordalivepress.ca

MIXTE
Papier issu de
sources responsables
FSC® C103567

Cataloguing in Publication information can be obtained from Library and Archives Canada.

CONTENTS

ACKNOWLEDGEMENTS

I would like to thank my daughters, family, and friends who supported me throughout the time of my divorce and in the writing of this book. In particular, I appreciate the prayers of Cath, Donna, Elaine, Eleanor, Irene, Lillian, Lorna, Lynette, and Wendy, as I wrote. Thanks to the team at Word Alive Press, who offered support and advice throughout the publishing process.

INTRODUCTION

Everyone has a 'story.' Mine is one of heartbreak, of going through two "divorces" at the same time! No doubt your details will be different, but I believe the lessons I've learned and share in these devotionals will help you as they have helped me. Right now, you may feel like your world has fallen apart. But I have good news. God can help you rebuild a beautiful life.

The Bible gives us several examples of such rebuilding. The prophet Isaiah shared a wonderful message of hope with the remnant of Israel. They had survived the Babylonian exile and cruelty and were working hard to rebuild their lives and community. But things weren't going well, and some began to wonder if God even cared. Isaiah gave them the encouraging message that He really does. God demonstrated their value to Him by writing them on the palms of His hands and telling them their protective city walls were always on His mind, always His concern (Isaiah 49:16).

As He did with Israel, God will provide you with a "crown of beauty," "oil of joy," and a "garment of praise" instead of depression and sadness just as He did in Isaiah's day (Isaiah 61:3). The next verse is the inspiration for the title of this book:

*And they will **rebuild** this place from its ancient ruins;*
*they will **restore** the ages-old, once-splendid structures;*
*They will **renew** Israel's ruined cities from the ashes and debris that*
laid untouched for many generations.
(Isaiah 61:4, VOICE) (bold emphases mine)

Another reference to rebuilding can be found in the book of Nehemiah. His memoirs became my guide for rebuilding my own life. They also form the backbone for this book, and you'll find references to his story throughout these pages.

I enjoy watching make-overs, particularly home renovations. Throughout these devotionals, you'll find similarities between rebuilding your life and rebuilding a house or a city wall, as was the case with Nehemiah.

This book has been years in the making. It's not only my story, it also includes lessons I learned from others along my healing journey. My first encounter with divorce happened when one of my sisters moved back home with two young children. I was about fourteen, and divorce was something you didn't talk about. Since then, I've observed and spoken with other Christians who have experienced divorce—family, friends, and acquaintances from various denominations and my workplace. The chapters of my divorce are many, and I also participated in a divorce support group and read many books and blogs.

Although I'm certainly not an expert in the field, I believe God called me to write this book. As I considered various topics, I felt conflicted within myself. *Should I expect others to do what I had not yet completed?* But the encouragement from the Lord and close friends was, "Write it anyway!" Writing this has been a blessing and helped me to grow deeper in Christ. I hope reading it will be a blessing and benefit to you as well.

This book provides the guidelines and the architectural plans. Are you ready to start rebuilding?

VISIONS OF THE FUTURE

My heart ached, and the tears flowed. Life wasn't supposed to happen like this! My husband had left me and our two girls less than a week before.

It was January 1, 2000, but I wasn't celebrating. Instead, I began a journal: "Here it is the beginning of a new year, a new decade, a new century, a new millennium! I've just watched the Rose Bowl Parade. The theme this year was 'Visions of the Future.'"

Life had taken a turn, and my "Visions of the Future" were bleak at that moment. Yet, I believed in God and knew He cared about my present and future.

READING:
Jeremiah 29:10–14

Today's reading from Jeremiah is about God's encouragement to His chosen people. They had been exiled to Babylon by King Nebuchadnezzar and lost their homes, jobs, and freedom. Separated from family and friends, their situation seemed impossible, yet God lovingly spoke words of hope and gave them a gracious promise of restoration. And these words from our Heavenly Father are still the same today.

That New Year's Day, I continued to journal: "Sometimes I feel optimistic that I'm going to make it—I'm going to be a much better person because of my experiences. I'm going to use them to help me grow, understand people better, and help others in their circumstances as well… I want to learn as much as I can about life and the Bible and to someday write about what I've learned…."

When our 'Visions of the Future' include our Heavenly Father's promises, hope and a future are ours, beyond what we could ever imagine!

As I begin this journey, Lord, help me never to forget You hold my future; You are watching over me, and You care about me. I put my trust in You. Amen.

What a God we have! And how fortunate we are to have him, this Father of our Master Jesus! Because Jesus was raised from the dead, we've been given a brand-new life and have everything to live for, including a future in heaven—and the future starts now! God is keeping careful watch over us and the future. The Day is coming when you'll have it all—life healed and whole.
(1 Peter 1:3–5, MSG)

Journaling Your Journey

READING:
Psalm 77:1–15

...I will remember the deeds of the Lord; yes, I will remember your miracles of long ago. I will consider all your works and meditate on all your mighty deeds.
(Psalm 77:11–12)

The idea of journaling terrified me. I had never done it before, and I didn't want anyone to find my book and read my thoughts. But I did start, and although it's not day-to-day writing (sometimes months passed between), it proved to be a reminder later of how far I had come.

The Bible contains many records and often lists the names of the recorders. For example, many of the Psalms, such as today's reading, are journals David and others wrote, expressing their thoughts and feelings to and about God, especially during difficult times. And aren't we glad they did!

As I journaled, I could literally see my thoughts, activities, frustrations, heartaches, joys, and things I was thankful for reflected in the words I wrote. It made me more aware of what was happening inside and around me. I began to see what was important to me, and to recognize the things that produce positive and negative reactions.

Sometimes I recorded thoughts about Bible readings, showing insights gained. I became more aware of what the Holy Spirit was telling me. It helped to strengthen and reinforce why I made certain decisions. It helped me to better understand why I reacted to certain things in specific ways. It also became a safe way to express my negative feelings without impulsively lashing out at others.

Journaling is an opportunity to record ideas, inspiring quotations, and answers to prayer. It's a way to remember children's cute sayings or other tender moments. You can write about positive things that will bring back pleasant memories and reminders of how God has helped you. Journaling will help you track your personal growth.

So why not pick up a pen and notebook and start today?

Lord, I find it so hard to express my thoughts and feelings. Thank You for Your understanding and for inspiring me as I write. Amen.

HITTING ROCK BOTTOM

Shortly after my husband left, I told my boss I needed a little time before returning to work. The response was, "Gladys, did you know your husband resigned?" I didn't and was told to talk to the CEO right away.

Because we had been in ministry together, the CEO said my husband's resignation included me and the papers were to be processed that afternoon. Frantic, I tried to contact the personnel director but couldn't speak with him for a few days.

Sitting in his office later, he handed me my "divorce papers" (aka pink slip). All I could utter was, "This isn't right!" He seemed to agree but had to follow procedures. There was nothing I could do. Although I didn't know it at the time, I had already received my final cheque.

How was I to tell the girls there would be no money coming in, medical/dental insurance, or grant for my older daughter's college degree? We were about to lose our furnished home and company car.

I filled in unemployment papers. It would be many weeks before receiving my first cheque, and I was directed to the welfare office. I couldn't believe what was happening. This was the organization I had worked so hard for and loved for years. They helped my dad when he needed it. Working with them, I had opportunities to help others through tough times. Now, they were putting me in this position. My mind was going in a thousand different directions.

Hitting rock bottom was the time I drew closer to God than I'd ever been. Although I had seen Him in action many times before, I wasn't prepared for what He was about to do. God has been beside me through the years, continually amazing me with big and little things, including the organization later allowing us to stay in the house for a few months while I looked for work. Although there were still more twists and turns on my journey, He has proven again and again that He is all I need.

READING:
Lamentations 3:19–26, 55–58

…You will be shocked and amazed. For in your days, I am doing a work, a work you will never believe even if someone tells you plainly!
(Habakkuk 1:5, VOICE)

Wondering how to rise from rock bottom? Look up! God is amazing!

Help, God—I've hit rock bottom! Listen to my heartache and grant me mercy (Psalm 130:1–2). There are no limits to what You can do, so I yield myself to You as my only hope and my Mighty Counsellor. Amen.

A TIME TO MOURN

Just a few months later, a couple of days after our uncelebrated 25th Anniversary, there was a knock at my door. A man asked my name then handed me an envelope. Inside were divorce papers.

Upon hearing the news a few days later, our office president prayed with me and said, "Now it's time to start rebuilding your life." I left his office, remembering a Bible study I had conducted years earlier on Nehemiah. As I reflected on Nehemiah rebuilding the walls of Jerusalem, I related that process to rebuilding my life.

From the beginning of Nehemiah's memoirs, I could relate to his feelings. He had terrible news. One of the things that mattered most to him in life had fallen apart, and he sat down and wept. The walls of Jerusalem were in ruins, leaving the inhabitants open to ridicule and attack. The city was the laughingstock of ungodly neighbours because only a walled city was considered respectable.

However, Nehemiah remembered that God had chosen Jerusalem as a dwelling for His Name (Nehemiah 1:9), meaning God had chosen to identify the Holy City with Himself. Therefore, the condition of the walls reflected upon God's glory. They were essential to protect both the people and the temple from attack and ensure the continuity of worship.

In many ways, those broken-down walls represented my life. I was vulnerable and felt open to ridicule and attack. As a Christian, I felt my divorce had disgraced God's name and that it allowed non-Christians to poke fun at Christianity. I had lost my husband, home, job, respect, and self-esteem. Like Nehemiah, I mourned.

Destruction needs time for mourning. We need that time to heal. If you haven't yet grieved your losses, you need to do so. Let the tears flow.

READING:
Nehemiah 1:1–4

...a time to weep and a time to laugh, a time to mourn and a time to dance...
(Ecclesiastes 3:4)

After a time of grief, it's time to move on..God has promised His comfort and help. That alone should make you want to show off your happy dance!

Lord, You promised that those who mourn would be comforted (Matthew 5:4). *I claim that promise today. Amen.*

WHEN THE WORLD CRASHES IN ON YOU

Some days were more challenging. Like the day I lay in the fetal position on the bathroom floor, sobbing uncontrollably, hardly able to breathe. Then, finally, I cried out to God, "I… can't… do… this… anymore!"

I tried to be strong, to keep things together, yet there I was, on the bathroom floor, feeling like a failure, feeling like I just couldn't put one foot in front of the other.

My daughter was there, not knowing what to do or say. I hated her seeing me like that, trying my best just to breathe.

She got me up, hugged me, and took me to my room, all the time trying to assure me it was going to be okay; we would get through this. And do you know what? We did! Not in our own strength, by any means, but with God's help.

At some point, you'll come to the moment when you realize you can't continue in your own strength. You may have been strong in the past, and you may have even won a battle or two. But there comes a time when you realize you're just not winning the war. After giving it all you've got, you're just not making it through.

You may not be lying in the fetal position, sobbing until you can't breathe. But if you haven't already done so, stop trying to get through life in your own strength. Instead, turn everything over to God, who cares so much for you and is willing and able to bring you through.

God, I can't do this anymore on my own. So I fall before You, asking You to help me through this. I give You control of my life. Amen.

READING:
Psalm 118

… and provide for those who grieve in Zion— to bestow on them a crown of beauty instead of ashes, the oil of joy instead of mourning, and a garment of praise instead of a spirit of despair…
(Isaiah 61:3)

OH, FOR A SOUND MIND

READING:
John 11:17–44

For God did not give us a spirit of timidity or cowardice or fear, but [He has given us a spirit] of power and of love and of sound judgment and personal discipline [abilities that result in a calm, well-balanced mind and self-control].
(2 Timothy 1:7, AMP)

My sister, Lillian, and her husband, Murray, purchased a new home and were looking forward to moving in two days. While she was at work, Murray finished the last-minute packing. At noon, my sister received a phone call from a friend urging her to get home quickly. The friend had gone to help Murray with cleaning but found him dead on the sofa. Because it was a sudden death, the police were involved. Lillian had to wait months for the autopsy results to learn he had choked to death.

Amidst this sudden turmoil, Lillian had decisions to make. She could have said no to the move, causing a ripple effect for the other buyers and sellers involved. But she chose to go ahead, signing papers to release their house to the new buyers and signing papers at the bank for interim financing to finalize the purchase of her new home.

Months before this, she had purchased her ticket to go on a short-term mission trip following their move. This trip was only three weeks away, and she chose to go ahead with it. Reflecting back, she's glad. God helped her make those choices.

When we go through a crisis of any kind, we often have to make some of the most important decisions of our lives. As a result, we may feel emotionally unstable, fearful of what the future may hold. We're afraid of making the wrong decision and feel exhausted trying to figure out what to do.

If we let Him, God will take our fear and exchange it for power, love, and a sound mind. And He promises to guide us and give us wisdom in making those decisions.

Father, I have so many decisions to make. I'm tired and don't know what to do. Please help me to make the right choices. Amen.

ARE YOU A DO-IT-YOURSELFER?

David was on the run. This mighty man who had killed Goliath, this hero in the king's court, now feared for his life. This man of whom it was said, *"Saul has slain his thousands and David his tens of thousands"* (1 Samuel 18:7), now saw his life caving in around him.

David's wife had turned against him, and King Saul had tried to kill him several times. David ran to Samuel and his best friend, Jonathan, for help but kept running for his life. He fled to the city of Nob, where he desperately lied to the priest. The priest gave David the sword of Goliath, which should have reminded him to trust God just as he had when he'd killed the giant.

But no. The psalmist ran to Gath, Goliath's hometown, and tried to make friends with his enemies. That didn't work. He panicked, pretending to be insane until they let him go. He kept running—all the way to the caves.

When in Israel, I saw those caves in the rocky, barren wilderness. It's a lonely place with wild animals. David had done everything he could think of to get himself out of the fix he was in, and this is where it had gotten him!

Alone in the cave, David finally took refuge in the Lord. He let go and let God have control. It was here that he wrote Psalm 57.

It was into this very same cave that Saul came to "relieve" himself, and though he could have easily done so, David would not kill his king, choosing instead to wait for God to act. David didn't have to run or lie anymore. He didn't have to feel insane anymore. He didn't have to fight his battles in his own strength anymore.

When life is caving in around us, tempting us to do wrong and handle things ourselves, we can turn to God, our refuge.

Are you a do-it-yourselfer? What appears to be a good solution may do more harm than good. Ask God what He

READING:
1 Samuel 21:1–15

...I will take refuge in the shadow of your wings until the disaster has passed.
(Psalm 57:1)

wants you to do and when. His timing is best. When you're tempted to jump in and get things moving, don't cave in as David did.

I cry out to You, God: I run to You for dear life. You always do what is right for me, so I ask You to help me now. Amen.

VIEW FROM A HELICOPTER

I turned the corner just in time to see a car heading straight toward me. I pulled over to avoid a collision, but the next thing I knew, my glasses went flying. I felt the sideways jolt, saved by my seatbelt. I soon knew I was severely injured.

Eventually, a police officer arrived to check on me. A fireman had to cut the door off the car. I was placed on a backboard and rolled into the back of an ambulance.

The other driver was in the wrong lane, drunk, and going twice the speed limit. He hit the side mirror on another car, sending him like a bullet into my driver's door. Then he veered across the intersection, hitting some parked vehicles. I didn't know it, but a news helicopter flew overhead just after the paramedic closed the ambulance doors. The six o'clock news shared my fate with those who watched.

A day or so later, I checked the Internet to view the newscast. Unfortunately, it was no longer available, but I still found some footage. I had no idea so many emergency vehicles had shown up at the scene. In the video, lights lit up the night sky from the ambulances, fire trucks, and police cars. The entire scene stretched a whole city block.

Viewing the footage was almost surreal. As I saw the ambulance moving down the street, I realized that I was the person inside it.

But at the same time, the video gave me a sense of peace. While experiencing the accident, all I had been able to see was what was immediately around me—broken glass, a dented side door, and a few first responders. Seeing this footage made me realize that God could see much more. He had been aware that the accident was going to happen. He'd known what my family and I would have to endure, but He had seen a reason to allow it.

So often, in our own little world, we forget that God sees the big picture. And even though we don't understand His

READING:
Psalm 121

From heaven the Lord looks down and sees all mankind; from his dwelling place he watches all who live on earth—
(Psalm 33:13–14)

reasons at the time, He doesn't allow anything to happen to us that He can't bring us through.

> *Thank You, Lord, for not sleeping. Thank You for always being there for me and knowing what's going on in my life. Amen.*

HOW LONG?

There's a building boom going on in my area—houses, apartments, and condos are springing up everywhere. However, some buyers often end up disappointed at how quickly they were 'slapped' together. It seems many builders prefer quantity over quality.

As you begin rebuilding your life, it's not crucial that you get better fast, but rather that you get better.

When going through a divorce, an illness, or any other crisis, we want to know how long it will be before we feel better. Often people who have never experienced divorce think you should just have a good cry and then get on with your life. Others believe that the first year is the hardest, and everything will be okay after that. Some think you should start dating again to get on with your life without realizing that you may still need a lot of healing.

The time it takes varies from situation to situation. So much depends on the reasons for the divorce, how long you were married, your relationship with your ex-spouse, personalities, children, if you need to move or change jobs, finances, if court procedures are necessitated, and many other factors. For me, it was about five years, which seems to be about average for the length of time we were married. But don't compare yourself to me or anyone else. Divorce is the death of a marriage, and just as everyone handles their grief differently, everyone will recover from divorce on their own timetable. The key is always to move forward, even if it seems slow.

Days will come when you're feeling better, and then you'll see or hear something that brings back memories, and the pain will return. But eventually, as you look back, you'll see progress being made.

Don't get discouraged if things seem to be moving slower than you would like. Remember the fable of the

READING:
Psalm 13

...Though outwardly we are wasting away, yet inwardly we are being renewed day by day.
(2 Corinthians 4:16)

13

tortoise and the hare? It was slow and steady that won the race. Aim for quality, not speed. Be patient. Take things slowly but surely.

Lord, remind me to be "joyful in hope, patient in affliction..." (Romans 12:12). *Amen.*

HEALING TAKES TIME

Novelist Margaret Atwood has said, "A divorce is like an amputation: you survive it, but there's less of you."[1] A lot of healing is required, and as with anything, you will want the best care.

The process may involve pain, rest, rehabilitation, and a long recovery time. If you get up and go faster than you're supposed to, you could have a relapse and make things worse.

After the car accident, I needed surgery. Time itself wouldn't heal my wounds. I had to choose what to do while that time passed:

- Trust my doctor – I hadn't experienced this type of surgery before, but the doctor had previously performed it and knew what he was doing.
- Listen to my doctor – So, too, we must listen to God, our Great Physician and do what He says (James 1:22).
- Rest – Hard as it was at times, I had to take time to rest and relax, so I didn't tear out the stitches or cause more harm. As we see in today's reading, when we come to Christ, He will give us rest.
- Take my medicine – It helped with the pain and prevented infection. So often, when it comes to our emotional well-being, we will have some 'bitter pills' to swallow, but the result brings healing.
- Let others help – My family and friends took care of me and most of my household tasks. No matter how independent we may be, there are times we need the support of others to help us through the healing process.
- Not pick at the wound – This can cause even more pain and take longer to heal.

What you face may not be something you will quickly get over, but in time healing will come.

Throughout your day, I hope you will reflect on this "prescription."

READING:
Matthew 11:28–30

By faith in the name of Jesus, this man whom you see and know was made strong. It is Jesus' name and the faith that comes through him that has completely healed him, as you can all see.
(Acts 3:16)

God, my life has been ripped apart, and it hurts. You promised to heal the broken-hearted and bind up their wounds. Help me trust You as my Great Physician and do my part in my restoration. Amen.

A Journey of a
Thousand Miles

I watched my granddaughter take her first step. After she got the hang of it, you couldn't hold her back. She ran around the house, climbed the stairs, and, after all these years, she is still always on the go.

What if she hadn't tried to take that first step?

You have a long journey ahead of you to rebuild your life, but as the old saying goes, "A journey of a thousand miles begins with a single step."[2]

Here are some essential steps in the healing process:

1. Point yourself in the right direction—towards God.
2. Face the facts. You may not want to face the truth about your divorce, and you may feel too exhausted emotionally to take this step. However, with God's help and strength, you can do it.
3. Understand that you must go through the healing process. You will not wake up tomorrow and find this all behind you.

READING:
Proverbs 4:11–15

Yes, you have a long journey ahead of you. People will tell you to get over it and get on with your life. But building takes time, effort, and wisdom if you want it done right. Step by step, you will find healing. The walk won't be easy, but you're not alone. The psalmist said: *"The Lord makes firm the steps of the one who delights in him; though he may stumble, he will not fall, for the Lord upholds him with his hand"* (Psalm 37:23–24).

Are you following God's lead and holding His hand?

Heavenly Father, I want to hold Your hand as I take each step. Point me in the right direction and walk with me every step of the way along the path You have set out for me. Lift me when I fall. I trust You and will take that first step today. Amen.

I carefully charted out my paths to align my steps with Your decrees.
(Psalm 119:59, VOICE)

WHEN ALL IS DARK

It was the darkest place I had ever been. I felt my young daughter slip her hand into mine as I stood there. We were part of a coal-mine tour in Glace Bay, Nova Scotia. These mines extended several miles under the ocean. For a moment, the tour guide had the lights turned off, and you couldn't see your hand in front of your face.

As we moved further into the mine, we saw a bright light—a fluorescent one, actually—which led us to a beautiful garden of pure, white lilies, growing because of the light.

Sometimes we may feel like we're in the darkest pit anyone has ever seen, like nothing good will ever happen to us again. Yet, we can have hope. The One who is the Light of the World—Jesus Christ—can pierce that darkness and cause good things to start happening in unexpected places.

Against the dark sky, stars shine their brightest. Against a dark background, jewellers display the beauty of diamonds. Despite the fear and darkness in which Jeremiah (the author of Lamentations) found himself, he reached out and grabbed hold of that one gem of truth—God doesn't cast off His people forever. He will show compassion. You can trust Him.

Throughout your day, look for beauty against a dark backdrop. Meditate on how God envisions you. And remember, no matter how dark it gets, the sun will rise again.

Thank You for being merciful and gracious to me, Father. I take refuge in You, and by faith, I know I can rejoice in these dark times because You care about me, and You hold my hand through these days. Amen.

READING:
Lamentations 3:1–26

He has driven me away and made me walk in darkness rather than light…
Yet this I call to mind and therefore I have hope: Because of the Lord's great love we are not consumed, for his compassions never fail. They are new every morning; great is your faithfulness.
(Lamentations 3:2, 21–23)

FALSELY ACCUSED

The story of Joseph inspires me. He had been torn away from his family, disowned by his brothers, made a slave in a foreign country, falsely accused, and imprisoned. What terrible injustice. Most of us would have probably become bitter against our family, accusers, and God, who allowed all this to happen. Yet through it all, even in prison, Joseph trusted God, and the Lord was with him even in jail (Acts 7:9).

God was preparing Joseph for more significant work than he could have imagined. God rewarded his faithfulness, giving him the ability to interpret dreams, and it was this ability that took him from prison to power.

It's difficult enough to suffer when it's our fault. But to suffer because of the adverse effects of someone else's decision is more challenging. Joseph had every reason to blame his suffering on his brothers and Potiphar's wife. But he didn't. Instead, we find that he

1. kept a clear conscience—demonstrating his innocence by living a good life despite the unfairness;
2. kept doing his best—preparing himself for the task God had for him, even though he didn't know what that was at the time; and
3. kept practicing God's presence—remembering He was with him, praying, and consciously relying on God.

God doesn't guarantee others won't treat us unjustly. But He does ensure His presence.

Joseph could have bitterly relived the pain his brothers brought upon him or how Potiphar's wife lied about him. He could have become a victim of negativity. But, instead, with God's help, he chose to forget.

Will you follow Joseph's example?

Even in this challenging place in my life, Lord, help me know You are with me, reaching out in kindness. I trust You to use these circumstances to bring blessings to me and to others. Amen.

READING:
Genesis 39:1–21

We are cracked and chipped from our afflictions on all sides, but we are not crushed by them. We are bewildered at times, but we do not give in to despair. We are persecuted, but we have not been abandoned. We have been knocked down, but we are not destroyed.
(2 Corinthians 4:8–9, VOICE)

GRIEF IN GETHSEMANE

READING:
Luke 22:39–46

An angel from heaven appeared to him and strengthened him.
(Luke 22:43)

From childhood, I had wanted to visit the Holy Land. After we married, I dreamed of going there for a second honeymoon. So we were thrilled to be chosen for a free trip to Israel a few months before our 25th Anniversary. But as the time came near, my dream became more of a nightmare!

During those months, my husband was being enticed in another direction. I tried to keep our marriage together, and my counsellor, some family, and close friends joined me in praying. We were sure if he went on this trip, it would turn his life around, save our marriage, and we would live happily ever after. It may happen in fairy tales, but it didn't happen to us.

We went on the trip, although he didn't talk much. As the days passed, it looked more and more like our marriage was over. Toward the end of the tour, our group was in the Garden of Gethsemane. Remembering the words of Jesus, I too prayed, "Father, take this cup from me; yet not my will but Yours be done." But, like Jesus, the 'cup' wasn't taken from me.

Jesus knew what lay ahead of Him. As our tour continued, we saw the prison dungeon where He was kept during the trial. We walked the Via Dolorosa, the road where He carried His cross and visited the Place of the Skull, where He was crucified. Much more than the physical torment He faced, Jesus had the awful prospect of bearing the sins of the world. In His humanity, Jesus didn't want to suffer. And God the Father didn't stop it!

I hope you didn't miss the little verse tucked away in the story—today's thought from Luke 22:43. If you're facing suffering, and it seems God isn't stopping it, know that Jesus knows what it feels like when the Father allows you to go through such hard times. But, as with Christ, He won't leave you alone but will strengthen you through it. And in the end, it will bring honour and glory to Him.

Father, keep reminding me that You said not to fear or be dismayed because You would strengthen me, help me, and uphold me with Your victorious right hand (Isaiah 41:10). *Amen.*

TRUST THE ARCHITECT

I trusted my husband, and he let me down. I trusted the Christian organization I worked with, but they let me down when I needed them the most. I had prayed earnestly and believed that God would answer my prayers for our marriage, but it still fell apart. *Where was God?* He had come through for my family and me so many times before. *Why didn't He answer my prayers? Could I still trust Him?*

As I read my Bible, I came across the story of Eve being tempted in the Garden of Eden. The serpent challenged the thought that she could trust God, and she fell for it. Of course, I didn't want to do the same thing. But, even though I didn't understand His reasons for not granting my request, I knew that He was more reliable and trustworthy than anyone else. So I hung on, despite my questions. And He never failed. Repeatedly, He proved that I could trust Him to do what's best.

My grandfather was an architect, and although I was quite young when he died, I've seen many of the structures he designed and built. Perhaps that's one of the reasons why I have such an interest in design and rebuilding. I thought of God as the Architect of our lives and wondered how this relates to architects today. So here are ten things I learned.[3] They provide a wealth of knowledge, design with you in mind, offer peace of mind, provide project administration, act as your advocate, guide you, work with qualified professionals to do the best job for you, make sure the design fits into the surroundings, have a clear vision of the result, and provide open lines of communication.

I'm glad I chose God as the Architect to rebuild my life. Will you trust Him with yours too?

Father, right now, I don't know who to trust, but the more I learn about You, the more I want You as my Architect. So I turn over my rebuilding project to You. Amen.

READING:
Psalm 28

Place your trust in the Eternal; rely on Him completely; never depend upon your own ideas and inventions. Give Him the credit for everything you accomplish, and He will smooth out and straighten the road that lies ahead.
(Proverbs 3:5–6, VOICE)

WHITE-OUT CONDITIONS

I spent a good part of my life on the Canadian Prairies. Windstorms weren't uncommon, especially in the winter when, all of a sudden, you could find yourself driving through blinding snow—white-out conditions where you couldn't see as much as a car length in front of you.

That picture came to mind when I read a story shared by James W. Moore in his book *When the World Takes the Wind Out of Your Sails*. It's the story of Hans, a shepherd boy. One winter afternoon, Hans was leading the sheep home from the mountain. Suddenly, he found himself in a vicious snowstorm. His first instinct was to turn around and head away from it. But then he remembered something his father had taught him—if you're ever caught in a snowstorm, head straight into it. That seemed like strange advice, and Hans couldn't remember why his dad had said to do this.

Knowing his father was a wise shepherd, Hans trusted his advice, even though it seemed ridiculous. He drove his sheep into the face of the storm, despite their reluctance. It was hard, painful, and frightening, but Hans kept on going.

Finally, they got through the worst of the storm, and his father and brothers were there to help him. Hans told his dad he took his advice, but he didn't understand why he had to face the storm. Trying to run away from it seemed better.

"'If you had,' his father said, 'it would have been disastrous. The wind would have blown the fur of the sheep upward, and the snow would have gotten in and formed ice, and the sheep would have frozen to death...'"⁴

You are heading straight into the storm of a divorce. But just as with the sheep, remember—it never pays to run away. Instead, trust God to lead you through it.

Father, I pray You will bring me through the storms I will face going through this divorce. Help me trust You in every situation, even when I don't understand Your reasoning. Amen.

READING:
Psalm 31:19–24

Some trust in chariots and some in horses, but we trust in the name of the Lord our God.
(Psalm 20:7)

FOLLOWING THE BLUEPRINTS

I'm not sure if it was because of the events of the eighteen months after the divorce, a mid-life crisis, or a combination of them both, but I started to examine my life.

A couple of things got me thinking. First, one of my co-workers shared in devotions about leaving a legacy for his children. Second, a few weeks before that, someone I knew died of cancer in her forties, and the church at her service was packed! So I began thinking about the impact I was making on the world and what I wanted to do with the rest of my life.

At that point, Rick Warren's book *Purpose Driven Life* became popular, and I began to read it. I realized that my primary purpose of serving God full-time hadn't changed; it was just the location and method that was different.

At work, we had talked about mission statements. Most organizations and businesses have one, setting a goal and finding ways to achieve that goal. Goals give direction and purpose to what we're doing. They're a measuring tool to see how far we've come and a reason to celebrate once we've reached them.

The Apostle Paul knew what he wanted to do with his life. He recorded his far-reaching goal in Philippians 3:14, and every day he moved closer toward it.

God provided us with His blueprints in the Bible. He has set goals for us and has given us His promise to help us reach those goals. Though we will never attain perfection on this earth, we, like Paul, must keep pressing on.

Take some time today to think about what you want to accomplish in your lifetime. Is God in agreement? What do you need to do today to start reaching that goal? What do the blueprints look like as you rebuild your life?

God, help me set goals according to Your will for me. Then, help me to move ahead each day in reaching them. Amen.

READING:
Proverbs 19:20–21

I am sprinting toward the only goal that counts: to cross the line, to win the prize, and to hear God's call to resurrection life found exclusively in Jesus the Anointed.
(Philippians 3:14, VOICE)

LEAVING NO STONE UNTURNED

READING:
2 Corinthians
13:5–10

Pay close attention to yourself [concentrate on your personal development] and to your teaching; persevere in these things [hold to them], for as you do this you will ensure salvation both for yourself and for those who hear you.
(1 Timothy 4:16, AMP)

Suppose you're doing a home rebuilding project. What about that flooring? Does it need a good sanding and staining, or does it need to be replaced? Will you remove a wall to open things up? Will you keep those cabinets? Could they be used in another part of your home? Do they need to be repainted first and perhaps have new handles put on the doors?

When Nehemiah and his workers rebuilt the wall, I'm sure they looked at every stone to determine what they could and couldn't use. Then, they likely turned them over to see if they merely needed to be cleaned up or if they needed to be chiselled, sanded down, and made to fit.

As we continue to work through these devotionals, we'll examine some of the debris often left from divorce. We'll also look at many "stones" worth keeping, but that may need some work.

As you read these devotionals each day, take a few moments to journal the things God reveals to you, things that need to be a part of your rebuilding process. Then, at the end of the ninety days, review your journal and ask God to help you leave no stone unturned. Ask Him to show you where you need to start. That place will be different for each of us. The time and the methods used to prepare *your* rocks may be unlike how God worked in *my* life, but He wants us all to examine ourselves and hold on to only the things that will make our spiritual lives strong.

Father, I look around me and see so much of my life that has fallen apart, and I'm so tired and scared, but I don't want to stay in this mess any longer. So help me sort through the pieces and show me what You want me to build on and what I need to get rid of. Amen.

FILLING THE TOOLBOX

Although Nehemiah lived and worked in the king's palace, everything belonged to Artaxerxes. Nehemiah had nothing to rebuild the wall, but he knew the king had the resources to help.

During his months of prayer, the Lord revealed to Nehemiah what he would need. Then, with God's help, tact, and courtesy, Nehemiah invited Artaxerxes to join him in the project. He needed a sabbatical, safe passage, provisions along the way, and building materials. It was all granted to him!

Sometimes when we have needs, we're afraid to ask the right people. But, just as Nehemiah found Artaxerxes more interested and approachable than he thought, God can answer our prayers when we ask others for help.

Although Nehemiah worked hard on his petition to the king, he didn't take credit for getting the needed supplies. Instead, he saw it as evidence that God was with him and was gracious to him. No doubt he thanked the king for what he had done, and we should thank those who helped us. But when our requests have been preceded by earnest prayer, we acknowledge the help is evidence of God's grace.

Is your toolbox empty? What kinds of things do you need to rebuild your life? Take the time to pray about it. Remember, God owns every plant and animal, every bit of oil, every gem, every drop of water, piece of land, the planets, sun, moon, and stars. Angels are at His beck and call. He will see that you get everything you need.

Lord, help me remember You will meet all my needs. Every day You bless me with Your mercy. Amen.

READING:
Nehemiah 2:1–9

We use our powerful God-tools for smashing warped philosophies, tearing down barriers erected against the truth of God, fitting every loose thought and emotion and impulse into the structure of life shaped by Christ. Our tools are ready at hand for clearing the ground of every obstruction and building lives of obedience into maturity.
(2 Corinthians 10:4–6, MSG)

FINDING RESOURCES

Whenever I begin a new project, one of my first steps is to look at my resources. What is available? Then, as I move along, I often find new assets. And I found that's the way it was in rebuilding my life.

Portions of the Bible began to take on new meaning, as did many old hymns and worship songs. I started underlining words that meant a lot, and sometimes I would write in my journal how certain words took on new life. People recommended certain types of books and sometimes made them available. Many other books have since come into my possession. They have continued to be a source of learning; some are noted at the end of this book.

READING:
Exodus 4:1–11

And my God will meet all your needs according to the riches of his glory in Christ Jesus.
(Philippians 4:19)

I made a list of things I needed to rebuild my life and asked God to help me prioritize it. I prayed He would show me who could help me with specific areas, such as those who helped me invest for retirement. I looked around my family, workplace, and church and started naming those who could guide me in other areas. I started a ladies' book club at church and found their wisdom, prayer, and support invaluable.

I remember one time in our weekly devotions at work, a co-worker spoke on today's reading. He also told of David, who had five stones and the little boy, who had five loaves and two fish. God took what they had to meet needs and glorify Him. The co-worker asked what we had in our hands metaphorically. I literally had a pen in my hand, which I used for writing and frequently used for editing. God has often helped me use that pen to meet needs and bring glory to Him.

In today's reading, Moses felt inadequate, but the Lord reminded him He had given him all the resources he needed. The same is true for you.

Look around. What do you have in your hand? Who can help you find what you need?

Lord, You promised to supply all my needs, and I ask You today to show me what resources You have given me to get through this divorce. Amen.

The Power Tool of Prayer

It was some time after the car accident that I had to come face-to-face with the other driver's lawyers. Following a nerve-wracking rush-hour trip to the building, I made my way to the proper floor. After a quick washroom trip, I checked in. My nerves were raw as I met with my lawyer and swore my oath on the Bible. Then we found out the assigned boardroom had been double-booked. As the lawyer left to tend to those matters, my head started spinning with the activity around me.

I quickly texted my girls to let them know how it was going, and they immediately responded with, "Praying for you, Mom!" Tears flooded my eyes as peace, like a warm blanket, enveloped me.

My lawyer soon returned, and we made our way to the designated room where I was seated in front of a microphone and was told the proceedings would be recorded. Two lawyers sat opposite me, drilling me on every aspect of the accident and my injuries. My lawyer sat beside me, having assured me he would step into the conversation as needed.

After two-and-a-half hours of questioning, my lawyer asked for a break. As he walked me out, he said, "I've never had a client so calm in there as you!"

No matter what may come your way or wherever you are, never underestimate the power of prayer!

Father, help me remember to pray about everything and tell You how I feel. But then help me leave it with You to do what You know is best for me and be thankful for all You do for me. Then I can experience Your peace, which is beyond my understanding. Your peace will guard my heart and mind as I live for You (Philippians 4:6–7). Amen.

Reading:
Psalm 56

Pray always. Pray in the Spirit. Pray about everything in every way you know how! And keeping all this in mind, pray on behalf of God's people. Keep on praying feverishly, and be on the lookout until evil has been stayed. (Ephesians 6:18, VOICE)

You've Got the Power

One Thursday afternoon in August 2003, most of Ontario and several states lost electrical power. It only took nine seconds for a voltage fluctuation on a transmission line in Ohio to shut everything down.

The outage happened during the afternoon, and I was at a church camp in Ontario. We didn't think much about it until the sun started to set. Cars were driven close to the cabins so the lights could help lead the children to their rooms as they got ready for bed. Hours passed with no electricity; many of us started wondering how long this would last and what was happening to the food in our fridges and freezers at home.

READING:
Ephesians 1:15–23

...oh, the utter extravagance of his work in us who trust him— endless energy, boundless strength!
(Ephesians 1:19, MSG)

Thousands in the city were trapped in elevators and subways. Traffic lights were out of service; streetcars stood still. In Cleveland, 1.5 million people were without water because the backup power stopped at the treatment plant. Twelve major airports were shut down. Hospitals and nursing homes were all affected. There was no air conditioning during the heat of the day, and the outage lasted well into the weekend.

I also remember the ice storm of January 1998, one of Canada's most significant natural disasters. Power outages occurred, roads were shut down, thirty-five people died, 945 were injured, and 600,000 were displaced. More than 2.5 million people couldn't get to work, and many businesses had to close their doors.[5]

Mankind's power can fail, but God's power is always available, with no blackouts. It's the same power that raised Christ from the dead.

Rebuilding your life, especially after a crisis, can be a form of resurrection. It's like coming back from the dead. God has the power to raise us up, rebuild our lives, and help us enjoy life again.

Tap into His power today! You'll get a charge out of it!

God, sometimes I feel powerless. I want to tap into Your power and feel Your strength as You and I rebuild my life together. Amen.

YOU RAISE ME UP!

I've always had an interest in eagles. While going through a particularly rough time, I put a picture of an eagle by my desk along with the encouraging words of verse thirty-one from today's reading.

Eagles have a wingspan of about 1.5–2.5 metres (5–8 feet). They cruise at about 64 km/h (40 mph), but they can soar at 120–160 km/h (75–100 mph) when going after prey. Instead of flapping their wings, they rely on air currents to gain altitude.

Eaglets learn to fly by observing their parents. Born with an instinct called imprinting, they bond with the first moving object they see, following it until raised. They learn from a parent hovering over the nest, flapping its wings. As the fledgling stretches for food, it copies the parent, flapping its newly feathered wings. The wind created by the parent causes the eaglet to rise slightly above the nest while flapping its wings.

Then the parent stops feeding the eaglet, which stretches trying to reach food. Its muscles develop, and it loses baby fat until one day as the parent goes by, dangling food and causing an upwind, the tiny bird dares to fly for the first time. It glides through the air until it comes to a scrambling, tumbling stop on a nearby branch or stump. The parent drops the food nearby, and the eaglet pounces on it and is fed. This pattern continues for about a month until the baby has learned to climb with the winds and soar.[6]

If we are going to rise and soar like eagles, we, too, must learn from the best role model, Jesus Christ. He teaches us about life's pitfalls, and sometimes it seems He is withholding good things, but if we learn to *wait* upon Him, like the parent eagle, He will make us stronger and teach us to soar.

Father, I am weak on my own, but I am strong when I put my trust in You. So, I ask You to raise me up to be what You want me to be. Amen.

READING:
Isaiah 40:28–31

When your soul is famished and withering, He fills you with good and beautiful things, satisfying you as long as you live. He makes you strong like an eagle, restoring your youth.
(Psalm 103:5, VOICE)

THE AFTERMATH OF A STORM

READING:
Nehemiah
2:11–18

Our trouble is obvious: The wall of Jerusalem has been reduced to piles of rock, and its gates consumed by flame. Let us begin by rebuilding the wall of Jerusalem....
(Nehemiah 2:17, VOICE)

I was sitting in the entrance hall and heard the newscast. A tornado was coming. I saw the sky get dark. The winds picked up, hurling bits of debris through the air. Tree branches swayed, and the rain pelted down. Lightning flashed, and the claps of thunder were deafening.

Stunned, I saw a tree branch snap off, swirl through the air and shoot right through the window. Gasping and ducking, the rain pounded my face, my hair blowing in the wind. Although the chairs were fastened together and bolted to the floor, I felt them rocking back and forth. And then it was over! I was glad it was a tornado simulator and not an actual event!

A few months after our separation, I attended a divorce support group. There I heard going through a divorce was like going through a tornado.

You've probably seen pictures of the devastation left after a tornado, people wandering around what used to be their homes, picking up little pieces of mementoes that somehow managed to stay intact. They see things they have to walk away from that can't be replaced and things they know will need to be replaced with something new later.

That's how I picture Nehemiah surveying Jerusalem's destruction. He had come from a palace to now live in a pile of rubbish. But he didn't dwell on lingering over the negative situation. He examined it, determining what needed to be removed, what needed repair, and what needed to be replaced. Nehemiah decided what he needed in his toolbox, where and how to obtain the necessary materials, and who could help repair certain sections of the wall.

I hope you'll look at the situation in which you find yourself and see what in your life is worth hanging onto, what needs repair, what is to be cast aside, and who might be able to help you.

Father, teach me how to take a brief look at the mess I'm in and then keep my eyes focused on You. Amen.

FILLING CAVITIES

Have you ever had a cavity? You feel a little pain in your tooth and try to ignore it as long as possible. Finally, the day comes when you can't stand it anymore, and you try to get a rush appointment with the dentist, where you hear that whirring sound we all dread—the drill. The drill cleans out the tooth decay and creates a shape for the filling to bond to. The new filling rebuilds the portion of the tooth that was broken down by the decay.

Suppose the dentist cleaned out the cavity and then just left it. It wouldn't take long before you'd be in agony again.

Often, we need some stubble cleaned out of our lives—worry, fear, low self-esteem, unforgiveness, bitterness, and so on. Getting rid of these things can be painful, but getting rid of them isn't enough. They'll leave us with a cavity needing to be filled. If it's not filled with something good that will bring healing, then, just like the person in today's story, the empty space will be filled with even more evil things.

Little by little, as the demolition gets done, we can bring in the good things we want to have. But, of course, this doesn't necessarily happen all in one step. However, from time to time, over the months and years, as you rebuild your life, you'll notice that rot is being replaced with good things—out with the old and in with the new!

How is your makeover coming along?

Lord, sometimes I feel empty inside, and I know if I don't fill up on good things, then the dreaded decay from sin will fill up that space again. I hunger and thirst for Your righteousness. Please fill me today! Amen.

READING:
Luke 11:14–26

Blessed are those who hunger and thirst for righteousness, for they will be filled.
(Matthew 5:6)

Built by Wisdom

READING:
Proverbs 24:3–6

Suppose one of you wants to build a tower. Won't you first sit down and estimate the cost to see if you have enough money to complete it?"
(Luke 14:28)

My mind was going in a thousand different directions. There were so many decisions to be made, so much work to do. I often felt overwhelmed with everything, like there was just too much on my plate.

Then I thought, when I sit down to a big meal, I don't try to eat it all in one mouthful. I take a little at a time, chew on it, and swallow it before taking the next spoonful.

I developed a plan to take everything on my plate and break it down into bite-sized pieces. This helped me prioritize what needed to be done and gave me a sense of accountability. It visually showed me my progress and gave me a sense of direction rather than a feeling of chaos.

With binder in hand, I made a list of all the things I needed to do—get a job, figure out a financial plan, find a place to live, divide and pack our belongings, clean the house before moving out, to name just a few. Then, with God's help, I broke each topic down further, listing the order they should be done, thus developing a strategic plan. Next, I noted when each step needed to be accomplished and who or what I would need to achieve each task. Then I worked out the plan. It helped me focus on only one or two things each day.

At the beginning of the binder, I designed a page with the *Serenity Prayer* by Reinhold Niebuhr.[7] Those words became my daily prayer. There were things in my past that I couldn't change, as much as I wish I could, but I could change the way I felt about them and appreciate the lessons learned. On the other hand, there were things I could change, so I needed to look at what options I had to make those changes.

Perhaps today would be a good day to start cutting down everything on your plate into bite-sized pieces.

Right now, I'm feeling overwhelmed, and I don't see a way out of my circumstances. So show me how to see the challenges in my life as opportunities for You to show Your power. Amen.

A Solid Foundation

Having to travel to Turkey for work, God provided me with the funds to go on a short tour. I was amazed at the vast marble columns in ancient temples, such as the Temple of Artemis in Ephesus, one of the Seven Wonders of the Ancient World. The temple was made of marble except for the roof. It consisted of 127 columns, each eighteen metres (sixty feet) high. Today, only the foundations and a few sculptural fragments remain.

Imagine the weight the foundation had to bear. A strong foundation is essential. In rebuilding our lives, Jesus Christ is our foundation. He is our rock, our strength, and He does not shift like the sand.

Here are some ways to build up that foundation in our own lives:

- *The Word of God* – Each time Jesus was confronted by Satan, He said, "it is written" and quoted Scripture to refute the temptations. God's Word is our spiritual food, the way we grow strong. As we read, we need to pray that God will show us the meaning of what we read and how we can apply it. Distortions and half-truths will cause this pillar to become lopsided or fall short.
- *Prayer* – Let's look at some elements in the prayer Jesus taught His disciples: pray to God, recognizing Him for who He is; pray for His kingdom, that His will may be done in our lives, ask for daily needs to be met, for forgiveness, and to be kept from evil. The more you talk to God, the stronger you become as a Christian.
- *Faith* – Without faith, we wouldn't believe in our loving Heavenly Father; we wouldn't believe in a Saviour or the Holy Spirit to help us. Faith to a Christian is like mortar to a brick mason; it's the cement that holds everything together.

READING:
1 Corinthians
3:9–15

Let each carpenter who comes on the job take care to build on the foundation! Remember, there is only one foundation, the one already laid: Jesus Christ.
(1 Corinthians 3:11, MSG)

33

Tomorrow we will continue to look at how to build a firm foundation, but for now, ask yourself, "What kind of foundation am I rebuilding my life on?"

Lord, help me build on a sure foundation that can only come from building my relationship with You. Amen.

Underpinning for a Strong Foundation

While in Turkey, I was also amazed to see the various gods being worshipped. There were temples galore built to them, so much so that Paul wrote: *"For as I walked around and looked carefully at your objects of worship, I even found an altar with this inscription: TO AN UNKNOWN GOD. So you are ignorant of the very thing you worship—and this is what I am going to proclaim to you"* (Acts 17:23).

Here are more ways to build our foundation:

- *Worship* – When we worship the Lord, we become refreshed and at peace. How should we worship Him? With gladness (Psalm 100:2); in the splendour of His holiness (Psalm 29:2); with pure hearts (Isaiah 29:13); in spirit and in truth (John 4:24); offering ourselves as a living sacrifice (Romans 12:1); and, with reverence and awe (Hebrews 12:28).

- *Witness* – This is the ultimate expression of our faith. In Matthew 5:13–14 Jesus has called us to be the "light of the world," the "salt of the earth," and we aren't to shy away from telling or showing others how Christ is at work in us. That can sometimes be scary, but the Lord has promised to give us everything we need.

Witnessing begins at home, just as Lois and Eunice raised Timothy in the Christian faith (2 Timothy 1:5). Then, going into our communities, churches, and even into "all the world," we can show others the One in whom we trust. The results of sharing the gospel are left in God's hands, but we must be faithful in telling others about Him.

Are you building a solid foundation, living for Christ in all you say and do?

Lord, help me to be faithful in my worship of You and in witnessing to others about You. May they see You at work in my life. Amen.

READING:
Ephesians 2:19–22

With my mouth I will greatly extol the Lord; in the great throng of worshipers I will praise him.
(Psalm 109:30)

THE CORNERSTONE

READING:
1 Peter 2:4–8

See here, I am laying in Zion a stone, a tested stone—a cornerstone, chosen and precious—for a firm foundation. Whoever trusts in it will never be disgraced. Justice will be the line by which I lay out its floor plan, and righteousness will be My leveling tool. A hailstorm will pulverize and wash away the fraud and deception behind which people hide, and floodwaters will overrun their hiding place.
(Isaiah 28:16–17, VOICE)

I was thirteen years old when the church I grew up in built a new facility. I remember going to the "laying of the cornerstone." This seemed to be a happy occasion, but I couldn't understand what was important about unveiling a plaque on the exterior wall of the building. This plaque had the date of the ceremony and the special guest's name.

Much later, I learned the meaning of a cornerstone was much different in Bible times. Back then, people built their homes out of stone, so they knew the importance of the cornerstone: a rock specifically chosen for its beauty and strength. It sat at the corner of the foundation. All the other stones were measured and placed in reference to it, thus keeping the walls straight and stable. As a result, the building's design conformed to the cornerstone.

The Bible refers to Jesus as the Cornerstone. Paul writes, *"You are being built on a solid foundation: the message of the prophets and the voices of God's chosen emissaries with Jesus, the Anointed Himself, the precious cornerstone"* (Ephesians 2:20, VOICE). Not only does Jesus provide a secure foundation for our faith, but He is also precious because He has been tried and tested. Others may reject Him, but we can choose Him as the Cornerstone for our lives, the One who provides us with a solid foundation that keeps us going in the right direction.

Will you choose Jesus as your foundation and leader as you rebuild your life, or will you reject Him?

Jesus, I want You as the Cornerstone of my life. I need You as my foundation and the One I will follow because You alone can keep me going in the right direction. Amen.

SUPPORT BEAMS

God blessed me by surrounding me with supportive people. My new job had about twenty-five Christian employees from various denominations. Several had been divorced and knew something of how I was feeling. I often found an encouraging note on my desk, and friends were there to pray with me when I struggled.

When my daughter had to be in a hospital in downtown Toronto, an acquaintance from church offered to become my chauffeur. Through those hospital trips, we became good friends. She was someone I could talk to and bounce ideas off of. For example, she supported me in setting up and leading a divorce workshop. She also came alongside me to start a ladies' book club, which proved to be a wonderful, supportive group of friends. In addition, her husband helped me figure out my finances. An elderly lady at church would often just squeeze my hand and say, "I'm praying for you." Another wonderful Christian woman lived in the same apartment building, and she was there so many times for me to share a cup of tea or go for a walk as we chatted together.

Just as every building needs support beams, so do we as we rebuild our lives. We need people who will lift us up in prayer, listen to us, give us encouraging words, hold us accountable, and enrich our lives.

Here's a friendly thought—why not invite someone to join you today for a cup of coffee? You may just find yourself a support beam!

Father, lead me to quality friends who will help me build a stronger character and draw me closer to You— friends who will sharpen my mind, as iron sharpens iron (Proverbs 27:17). Help me to be faithful and trustworthy with them. Amen.

READING:
Mark 2:1–5

As long as Moses held up his hands, the Israelites were winning, but whenever he lowered his hands, the Amalekites were winning. When Moses' hands grew tired, they took a stone and put it under him and he sat on it. Aaron and Hur held his hands up… so that his hands remained steady till sunset.
(Exodus 17:11–12)

A WORD OF ADVICE

READING:
1 Kings 12:1–14

Listen to counsel, receive instruction, and accept correction, that you may be wise in the time to come.
(Proverbs 19:20, AMP)

Have you ever noticed people love to give advice? Just ask any new mother, someone who is ill, or a recent widow. Wise old Solomon told us to heed advice, but he also warned, *"the advice of the wicked is deceitful"* (Proverbs 12:5).

You will find many people who will advise you one way while others say the opposite, especially if you rely on social media groups who complain but rarely provide sound advice.

So how do we distinguish between good advice and bad? Let me give you a word of advice:

- Did you ask for God's direction?
- Does the advice agree with what the Bible says?
- Is the advisor trustworthy? Can you see how that person reflects good judgment? Are they good representatives of God's love, grace, and mercy? Do they continually seek to know God's will in their lives? Will they speak the truth in love? Are they good listeners? Will they keep what you say in confidence? Will they pray for you?

Rehoboam was Solomon's son, the king known for his wisdom and wealth. Instead of listening to the elders who served his father, Rehoboam followed bad counsel from his friends. He didn't consider the source of the counsel, nor did he compare it to what God had written. As a result, he lost his kingdom.

Whose advice do you listen to?

I praise You, Father, because You are the source of all knowledge. May Your Spirit dwell in me, helping me to discern good from evil so that I may do Your will. Amen.

Rebuilding Emotionally

My crisis brought on a whole avalanche of different emotions, which could change in a flash. Some I'd never felt before, or at least not to the same extent. That sometimes shocked me and others, and I didn't quite know what to make of it all. I was relieved to learn that these emotional responses are normal for people going through a divorce.

People would ask how I was doing, and rather than sharing how I felt, I would smile and say, "Good." I didn't want to let on that I felt lost, thinking they wouldn't understand or would blame me for not turning everything over to the Lord and getting on with my life. Sometimes I was too tired to talk about it, so it was easier to let on I was doing okay.

Ruth Stockdale, at that time Executive Director of Single Adult Ministry/SinglesLinc in Ontario, was one of the seminar leaders at the Divorce Education Workshop I organized. She had created and facilitated a divorce recovery program for several years, supporting hundreds of individuals through divorce recovery. For the promotional flyer, she e-mailed me the following to describe the workshop she was going to lead:

> Because of the flood of emotions that divorce can bring, a flood that usually results in confusion, it is critical that one recognizes that it is normal, and to emerge with confidence, it is necessary to come to an understanding of those emotions. Whether in the process of divorce or supporting another, emotional understanding is key as the emotions come and go unpredictably.

In rebuilding our lives, we need to process our emotions. It helps to have a trusted friend who will listen and still care. We all need to be heard! But in doing so, we must avoid downloading everything negative without also looking for

READING:
John 11:17–36

...And God will wipe away every tear from their eyes.
(Revelation 7:17)

39

something positive. We should remember our friends are not responsible for solving our problems or changing our emotions.

We have a choice—to process our emotions with God's help or react to them and let them dominate us.

Father, some days I feel so overwhelmed by my feelings. Help me to process them Your way rather than let them run my life. Amen.

OPPOSITION FROM WITHOUT AND WITHIN

Have you ever spent a wonderful time with the Lord only to have it followed by a challenging time? If so, you're in good company with Elijah, Moses, Jesus, and many others. In today's reading, we see this also happened to Nehemiah and his workers.

Sanballat was the governor of Samaria, just north of Jerusalem, and Tobiah was governor of Ammon, to the east. As a Jew, Tobiah had family living in Jerusalem. These men seemed to be highly regarded and talked others into discouraging those trying to rebuild the wall around Jerusalem and better their lives.

Sanballat and Tobiah and their friends made fun of the workers, saying the wall would tumble down if an animal like a fox walked on it. Nehemiah and his workers paid no attention and continued working.

There were also lies, threats, and evil plans, but the workers continued rebuilding while keeping guard. Nehemiah wouldn't let suppositions, exaggerations, hearsay, or gossip stand in their way. He didn't waste his time or breath trying to defend himself. He just kept on building.

If we continue reading in Nehemiah 5, we find friends and relatives of the workers taking advantage of a bad situation. There were financial issues to be faced, and the workers grew tired and frustrated to the point that they could no longer build. It got so bad they finally appealed to the authorities to straighten it out.

In Ephesians 6:10–17, we're told to put on our spiritual armour to fight against the devil's schemes—truth, righteousness, peace, faith, salvation, and the Word of God.

Did you put your armour on today?

Lord, You know that I feel disgraced and ashamed; You know that people scorn me (Psalm 69:19). So help me to stay focused on You in rebuilding my life. Amen.

READING:
Nehemiah 2:10–21

Be alert and of sober mind. Your enemy the devil prowls around like a roaring lion looking for someone to devour.
(1 Peter 5:8)

41

HEALING FROM THE INSIDE OUT

READING:
Ephesians 4:17–32

...take on an entirely new way of life—a God-fashioned life, a life renewed from the inside and working itself into your conduct as God accurately reproduces his character in you.
(Ephesians 4:24, MSG)

In my previously mentioned car accident, my leg was severely injured. I'll never forget a visit from my home healthcare nurse who came to check the wound. I told her about the pain, and as she examined the injury, there was significant discharge. She persisted in getting the pus out as I gripped the arms of the big chair I was sitting in. I was horrified. I saw a gaping hole and a significant dent in my leg. The nurse cleaned the area using an antiseptic and then packed the hole. I was told the leg would heal from the inside out; the cavity would get smaller and smaller until the skin again covered it over.

For many months, my wound needed daily care. The nurse would come to my home, pull off the old bandage, squeeze out all the pus (I can still feel the pain as I write this!), wash the hole with sterilized water, and rebandage it. It wasn't good enough to cover the wound with a bandage because the pus was collecting inside. The infection could have travelled throughout my body, causing irreparable damage.

I often thought about how much this reflects our lives. First, we have to eliminate the old decay that is causing us harm, then cleanse and sterilize so we can be filled with good things, allowing healing to occur from the inside out.

Today's reading reminds us we need to get rid of such things as anger, lying, gossip, bitterness, rage, and malice. These are all things that can grow inside of us—in our hearts and minds. They're the kind of things that can cause us harm and need to be cleaned out.

Cleaning out is a process that takes time, so perhaps you'll find making notes in your journal helpful as the Lord shows you what may be infecting your spiritual life. Then, as you pray, read, and allow God's Spirit to work over time, He will bring cleansing and healing.

Lord, I don't want anything in my life that isn't pleasing to You. So I pray that You will continue to work in me for as long as it takes. Bring healing in every area, from the inside out. Amen.

No Longer Disgraced

After my husband and I split up, I removed my wedding rings. Everywhere I went, I felt branded, like people were looking at my hands and noticing the rings were gone. I might as well have been walking around with a big "L" on my forehead; I felt like a loser.

Somehow, being married let the world know I was worthy of being loved by someone, but being divorced proved otherwise. I felt like I had let God down as well as the people to whom I had ministered for so many years.

When going through a divorce or feeling ashamed of things we've done, there is a solution. We no longer need to feel disgraced. It's not always easy, but when we seek God's forgiveness and allow Him to be our shield, glory, and hope, we can lift our heads and allow the shame to disappear. That's what the Psalmist David did.

Sometimes we're afraid to tell God exactly how we feel. We don't want to disappoint Him. But just like David, we can express our deep pain, frustrations, anger, and shame. He knows we're confused and often feel disgraced. David didn't mince his words; we can follow his example and tell God what we think.

We can ask God tough questions. That's what the prophet Jeremiah did when he said, *"Why was I ever born? To watch such tragedy? To feel such sorrow? To live my days in utter shame?"* (Jeremiah 20:18, VOICE). Depression is a natural response to loss. But thankfully, we don't need to dwell there.[8]

In your journal today, write about some of the losses you're experiencing. How does that make you feel?

God, sometimes I feel so ashamed, like such a disgrace. Help me to trust You for healing. Amen.

READING:
Isaiah 50:4–7

Because the Lord, the Eternal, helps me I will not be disgraced; so, I set my face like a rock, confident that I will not be ashamed.
(Isaiah 50:7, VOICE)

DID HIS BACK GET COLD?

READING:
Isaiah 53

There was nothing attractive about him, nothing to cause us to take a second look. He was looked down on and passed over, a man who suffered, who knew pain firsthand. One look at him and people turned away. We looked down on him, thought he was scum. But the fact is, it was our pains he carried—our disfigurements, all the things wrong with us.
(Isaiah 53:3–4, MSG)

I fumbled as I opened the box, unsure if I wanted to. For about twenty years, my nativity set had been a central part of our Christmas decorations. But it had now been years since I'd put it on display. I only kept it because my Mom had made it.

As I sat there, memories flooded my mind of that day, as they had every Christmas since my husband left. I recalled the day's tension and events that led up to him walking out the door with his suitcase. Sitting in the living room at the time, I happened to glance over at the nativity figurines on display. I felt ashamed and embarrassed that our marriage ended, especially at this time of year. While others were enjoying their family time, spreading love and good cheer, there I sat in tears.

Now, years later, as I prepared for Christmas, I carefully unwrapped each nativity piece and set them out before my daughter came with my three-year-old granddaughter. After they arrived, the toddler soon spotted them, and I showed her each figurine, telling her the Christmas story. She was fascinated by the manger, especially Baby Jesus lying there with just a "diaper." She turned the little figurine over and looked at the back, saying, "Did His back get cold?" I now have that precious new memory to think about when I set up my nativity set each year.

A more incredible blessing than my granddaughter's interest in the nativity set was that Jesus became a human and suffered physically and emotionally just like we do. Life wasn't easy for Him, either. But, of all people, He knows what it's like to be rejected.

Lord, help me remember today that You know what it's like to be in pain physically and emotionally. Thank You for being my Wonderful Counsellor, Mighty God, Everlasting Father, and Prince of Peace (Isaiah 9:6). Amen.

FEELING ALONE

I managed to get through the first year of our separation, which included my first birthday without my husband, Valentine's Day, our 25th wedding anniversary, and other special events. However, when I started hearing Christmas music and seeing window displays, I nearly fell apart. If I heard the carol, "I'll be Home for Christmas," I would have to turn it off or walk away.

Loneliness is hard to bear, and it's natural to feel lonely when going through a divorce. It feels like no one understands, yet feeling sorry for ourselves only leads to more discouragement and depression. A divorce recovery group can become like a family because of the shared pain.

Family and friends may sincerely want to help, but often they don't know what to say or how to interact with you, so they may pull away. You can't really blame them; you were probably there yourself before your own divorce. It's okay to be specific in explaining how they could help. But realize they also have their own responsibilities. Generally, people feel more comfortable knowing what to do. It's best to try to build friendships rather than tear them down.

Satan will use your loneliness to further separate you from others and God. The longer he can keep you separated from them, the more power he has over you. Think of ways to get to know more people. Seek out ways you can serve others who are lonely or in need.

Take comfort in knowing that your Heavenly Father has promised to always be with you. He even says that if we love Him and obey His teaching, He will make His home with us (John 14:23).

God, help me to remember that Immanuel means "God with us." You are faithful, and I ask You to refresh me again with Your hope and love. I invite You to come and dwell with me. Amen.

READING:
Psalm 25:16–22

I am like a solitary owl in the wilderness; I am a lost and lonely screech owl at home in the rubble. I stare at the ceiling, awake in my bed; I am alone, a defenseless sparrow perched on a roof.
(Psalm 102:6–7, VOICE)

FATHER, FORGIVE THEM

READING:
Matthew 6:9–15

*Jesus said,
"Father, forgive
them, for they do
not know what
they are doing."*
(Luke 23:34)

Forgiveness can be tough stuff. Oh, it's easy enough to forgive someone who accidentally bumps into us or forgets to return our phone call. But it can be a different matter when someone close deliberately hurts us!

Jesus had been wrongfully accused, tortured, and was near death. Crowds at the foot of the cross were laughing and taking in the scene. His accusers weren't repentant, still humiliating Him when He asked God to forgive them. For the most part, these were members of His beloved religion, people He may have worshipped with at the synagogue the Sabbath before.

It seems the more we know and love a person or group, the more we expect from them. But it's not common for them to know what to say or how to react when they learn of your divorce. It will hurt them to see you react and say things they haven't seen or heard from you before. They don't understand the wounds you're experiencing or how long it takes to heal. Sometimes they say or do things that make matters worse when they really intend to help. Often they don't know they've hurt you. Other times there may be gossip, and the rumours get back to you, adding to your hurt, especially when it comes from people you thought were your friends. Divorce is a messy experience for everyone, and you're caught in the middle of it all.

Forgiveness doesn't depend on the other person. Whether or not they are repentant or still accusing us, it's up to us to forgive. Not forgiving can lead to resentment and revenge. This is because our minds are controlled by bitterness instead of thinking about positive, helpful things.

Truly choosing to forgive someone doesn't come naturally, nor is it something we can always do in our own strength. But God can and will give us the grace to forgive those who have hurt us.

Father, help me to follow Your example of forgiveness. Give me the grace and strength I need, especially when _____ doesn't even care or notice how much I'm hurting. Amen.

BOUNDARY LINES

When we look at the wall built by Nehemiah and the Israelites, each gate spoke of some aspect of their lives, whether it was taking out the garbage, buying fish, going on a journey, preparing for worship, or conducting business. They would close the gates when it wasn't a good time for those various things, and they would open them when it was. Guards were placed on the wall to watch for approaching danger so the gates could be barred shut when necessary.

Just as the Israelites needed to protect their townsite boundaries, it is essential to protect personal boundaries. For example, you may find that your estranged spouse will "push your buttons," knowing what gets you angry and then blaming you for being an angry person. Or it may be a parent or someone else from your past who pushes you to act in the way *they* want. Watch for these signs so you can avoid them.

You may find that some people want you to be on track with them, not with God. So there will be lots of resistance to your boundaries and goals. Counselling (preferably Christian) can help you protect and develop your boundaries in a healthy way.

In the book *Secrets of Your Family Tree*, the various professional counsellors who authored the book list the following as personal things we should protect and take responsibility for: "thoughts, attitudes, opinions, beliefs, needs, choices, feelings, values, time, possessions, money, gifts, talents, behavior, and bodies."[9]

Do you need to start drawing some boundary lines?

Father, may my love grow more and more in wisdom and insight so I will be able to examine and determine the best from everything else (Philippians 1:9–10). *Amen.*

READING:
Nehemiah 3

...as for the upright, he considers, directs, and establishes his way [with the confidence of integrity].
(Proverbs 21:29, AMP)

FUEL FOR REVENGE

READING:
1 Peter 3:8–17

So put away your lies and speak the truth to one another because we are all part of one another. When you are angry, don't let it carry you into sin. Don't let the sun set with anger in your heart or give the devil room to work.
(Ephesians 4:25–27, VOICE)

One of the movies our family liked to watch was *The Princess Bride*. If you've seen it, you may recall the Spanish swordsman's famous quote, "Hello. My name is Inigo Montoya. You killed my father. Prepare to die."[10]

Watching him finally get his revenge may appear funny, but trying to get even is no joke in real life. Sadly, anger and frustration that lead to revenge are widespread in divorce. These days, quick responses are expected. So anger is often met with outrage, yelling is matched with screaming, hurtful words are acknowledged with even more hurtful words. Before reacting to a verbal rebuke, social media post, or phone message, take time to cool. If a response is necessary, kindness can go a long way. Tell them it's not a good time to talk about it now, and then get back to them once you've cooled off.

In his book *None of These Diseases*, Dr. McMillen tells of a study at one hospital showing "through personal interviews with patients suffering from mucous colitis, that resentment was the most prominent personality characteristic, occurring in ninety-six percent of the victims."[11] It can also cause high blood pressure, arthritis, and anger, among other problems. He adds that verbally running people down affects certain hormones from various glands, which can cause all sorts of diseases.

When we hate someone, they start controlling our thoughts. We find it hard to concentrate on anything else. The stress causes emotional fatigue; work becomes drudgery. We start taking out our frustrations on others.

Instead, maybe we should stop dwelling on what we think the other person or we deserve. Perhaps we should trust God more and let Him deal with the other person (Romans 12:19).

Lord, I ask for forgiveness for the harm I have caused and pray for help in making positive changes in my attitude. Amen.

STINKY GARBAGE

Many years ago, we lived in an old house that had become a breeding ground for spiders. They were everywhere. It became so bad we had to leave while it was fumigated. Then, upon our return, we had to open the windows and doors to let out the horrible smell. I wish I could say that was the end of it, but unfortunately, the scent lingered for a long time.

The worst was the residue. It permeated plastic bags, especially those containing stored items in the closets. For months, we would come across a hidden bag that reeked of that now-familiar stench. So many times, we had to toss out the bag, clean up the contents, and re-store them in another container.

While reading through Galatians 5 in *The Message* one day, I came across today's verse, which reminded me of the stench from the fumigation. It also made me think about how divorce's verbal and emotional garbage can become embedded in children. They may not be the target, but they still become contaminated, and it stinks for months, years, and sometimes decades. Life will never be the same for them, regardless of their age. Each child will handle the news of the divorce differently and cope in their own way. Often counselling is needed to help them get rid of the anger, fear, withdrawal, and depression that has overtaken them.

Amidst your own emotional upheaval, be aware that children (even adult children) may still love both parents and be desperate to find their place amidst the chaos that divorce often creates.

Father, my children are hurting and that hurts me too. Help me to deal with my own emotions in Your way so I can teach my children to follow my example. Guide my words, and help me find people and resources to help my children and me, so we no longer have to carry the burden of this stinky divorce. Amen.

READING:
Galatians 5:15–26

… a stinking accumulation of mental and emotional garbage…
(Galatians 5:20, MSG)

CHILDREN AS PAWNS

READING:
Psalm 36

The right-living act with integrity; the children who follow their example are happy.
(Proverbs 20:7, VOICE)

My granddaughter recently started playing chess. To play with her, I had to be reminded of the rules, what the pieces were called, and how they could be moved. The pawn is the weakest, with limited movement, and is often sacrificed to get ahead. In life, a pawn is a person or thing manipulated and used by others.

We've seen children treated this way by divorced parents. For example, one parent tries to discipline to be helpful, caring, and kind. At the same time, the other parent buys them everything they want, takes them to fun places, and lets them do whatever they want, knowing the other parent can't compete for their attention. Or one parent may be determined to make all the decisions when they're supposed to be co-parenting. We've even heard amber alerts where one parent illegally takes the child away or purposely keeps the child longer to spite the ex-partner.

Children learn from their parents. The way they see you act is how they will learn to treat others. The Bible teaches that children are to honour their parents in the Lord, so bad-mouthing the other parent goes against God's teaching. Your bad habits can damage your children: losing your temper, making it a power struggle with your ex, saying things like "that's just like your father," or "there she goes again; that's typical of your mother!"

Each child in a broken home will react differently. They may respond with anger, fear, or withdrawal. They may blame themselves. They may show signs of deep depression. But they can also survive and become healthy, mature adults. It takes hard work, staying connected to God, and developing support systems for yourself and your children.

Like pawns in a chess game, they can make it through, and they have the unique ability to become whatever they want, except for the king—that position is reserved for Jesus.

Father, teach me to model my life after Jesus, who was kind, compassionate, and loving, so my children can learn from my example. Amen.

RENEW AND RESTORE

No one person can be blamed for a divorce. There are at least two sides to the story. Could it be that the chaos is partly because of your lack of good judgment, trust, or sin? Perhaps others don't want anything more to do with you because of it. Maybe you've lost your family and your finances because of it. Perhaps no one knows except you and God!

After living successfully, King David's life collapsed. The psalmist, who loved the Lord and trusted Him, didn't join his army in battle. Instead, he got Bathsheba pregnant, had her husband killed, and then tried to cover it up. After being caught red-handed, Psalm 51 is his hymn of confession.

In this Psalm, David gives some insight into how he recovered. He didn't blame his parents, his wife, his church, or the devil—he knew that he alone was to blame for the mess he was in. So his confession wasn't just for public show, nor to elicit the sympathy of others; he owned up to his sin and wanted to change. He knew he had offended others, but ultimately, he had hurt God. His troubles began when he started leaving God out of his life.

David realized his real needs:

- To be cleansed and forgiven.
- To have his joy restored.
- For God to never remember his sins again.
- A new heart, meaning new feelings and emotions.
- A new sense of loyalty and faithfulness.
- God's presence in his life.
- The ability to use his past to help others.

David admitted he couldn't bring Bathsheba's husband back or undo his adultery. But he could, and did, humbly repent. God will be faithful to forgive and welcome anyone who comes to Him in repentance.

READING:
Psalm 51

Create in me a clean heart, O God; restore within me a sense of being brand new... Give back to me the deep delight of being saved by You; let Your willing Spirit sustain me. (Psalm 51:10, 12, VOICE)

You have all the facts before you... I've been out of step with you for a long time... What you're after is truth from the inside out. Enter me, then, conceive a new, true life... scrub me, and I'll have a snow-white life... God, make a fresh start in me. Amen. (Psalm 51, select verses, MSG)

SOMETHING BEAUTIFUL!

It was the second time I'd been to church since my husband had left. I wanted to leave the moment I looked at the Order of Service. We were going to sing Gaither's song "Something Beautiful," and I felt the lump forming in my throat. I noticed how sensitive I'd become to the words of certain songs and choruses—familiar things I'd sung before now took on new meaning. When we sang this song, I cried because it reminded me how my husband used to change one line and sing, "… He made something beautiful out of my *wife*."

I prayed that God *would* make something beautiful out of my life. But, I also cried because of the line, "All my confusion He understood…"[12] because I realized that even though I didn't understand, He did.

In her book, *Because He Lives*, Gloria Gaither talks about her three-year-old daughter, Suzanne, painting a picture. Accidentally, a big blob of black paint landed in the middle of her masterpiece. Suzanne tried to make something out of it as if the blob was supposed to be there; it didn't work. She got a cloth and tried to soak up the paint, rubbing the paper until there was a hole in it. She picked up the dripping piece, took it to her mom and sobbed, "I tried to make you something beautiful but just look! I dropped some paint… I tried to fix it, but it just got worse and now just look!"[13] Wiping her tears and hugging her little girl, Gloria gave Suzanne a new piece of paper to begin again.

Often our lives are like that painting. We have wonderful plans that we want to present to God, but somehow things get messed up. We try to patch them up ourselves but make matters worse. As we bring this confusion to God, He understands. And, in His mercy, He gives us a clean slate.

Father, help me not to give up but to remember that You are renewing my inner being every day. You can make something beautiful out of my life as I yield to You and trust You. Amen (2 Corinthians 4:16).

READING:
1 Peter 3:3–5

The Lord their God will save his people on that day as a shepherd saves his flock. They will sparkle in his land like jewels in a crown. How attractive and beautiful they will be.
(Zechariah 9:16–17)

RENEWING OF THE MIND

READING:
1 Corinthians
2:11–16

Finally, brothers and sisters, fill your minds with beauty and truth. Meditate on whatever is honorable, whatever is right, whatever is pure, whatever is lovely, whatever is good, whatever is virtuous and praiseworthy.
(Philippians 4:8, VOICE)

Going through a divorce certainly lowered my self-esteem. The person I had most trusted and loved threatened my self-worth. I felt like I wasn't worth his time or energy in trying to keep our marriage together.

Losing my job because of the divorce sent me a message—without my husband, I was worthless to the organization I loved and respected. I was a perfect candidate for the devil to swoop in with his lies and play havoc with my mind. I felt useless, unlovable, and helpless.

Those abused by their spouse in any way will experience many negative thoughts. For those who lost their spouse to someone else, the thoughts can be even worse—wanting to give the third person in the marriage a piece of your mind. Unfortunately, many think even less of themselves, wondering how bad they must be for their spouse to have an affair with someone who didn't even care that they were cheating.

The devil knows your weaknesses and where you're most vulnerable; your mind becomes a battlefield. It's not easy to stop believing the devil's lies. We must submit our thoughts to Christ. It may seem like forever before you realize that your self-esteem isn't based on what another person thinks but rather on how God sees you.

I had to again come to the place where I controlled my thinking, replacing bad thoughts with good ones. I got to choose. It's still an uphill climb at times, but God is helping to keep my mind focused on Him and on things He wants me to think about.

Having your self-worth threatened can be debilitating, but it's not hopeless. What do you think?

Lord, in Your power, help me to fight the thoughts the devil puts in my mind. May I be transformed by the renewal of my mind so I can discern Your will. Amen (Romans 12:2).

WHO AM I?

My identity had been so wrapped up in my husband and job I didn't know who I was anymore. I was no longer a 'Mrs.' or a 'pastor.' I had to change careers, and for three-and-a-half months, I looked for work, which isn't easy when you have no self-esteem and don't even know who you are anymore!

But God knew me and provided me with a good job in another Christian organization. I remember my first day there, walking down the hallway to my office and seeing my name outside the door. That's when I realized I was an individual, me, not a label.

My supervisor had a bouquet for me with a card that read: "Welcome to the national office. I'm so pleased you're joining our team! I look forward to getting to know you better and serving God with you in Communications." I started to get to know myself better too!

For people to know and understand me, I first needed to know myself. I began by going through my Bible and reading verses that told me who I am. I no longer wanted to be identified by human standards but by God who created me—a unique individual He chose to bring into this world as someone He would continue to love and care for (Psalm 139). He made me for a particular purpose (Ephesians 2:10). I am His child (Galatians 4:7, John 1:12), someone He cares enough about that He wants to make me more like Him, lacking nothing (James 1:4). I am someone He listens to (Psalm 34:5) and protects (Psalm 17:8–9). I am someone He loves so much that He sent His only Son to die for my sins (John 3:16). He made me His dwelling place (1 Corinthians 3:16).

He feels the same way about you!

Father, even though I sometimes struggle with who I am, I'm so glad You know all about me. Thank You for helping me to get to know me too! Keep reminding me when I forget how much You love me. Amen.

READING:
1 Peter 2:1–3, 9–17

...you also, like living stones, are being built into a spiritual house to be a holy priesthood, offering spiritual sacrifices acceptable to God through Jesus Christ.
(1 Peter 2:5)

HAPPY BIRTHDAY!

READING:
Psalm 139:13–16

*Your thoughts
and plans are
treasures to me,
O God! I cherish
each and every
one of them! How
grand in scope!
How many in
number! If I could
count each one of
them, they would
be more than
all the grains of
sand on earth.
Their number is
inconceivable!
Even when I wake
up, I am still near
to You.*
(Psalm 139:17–18,
VOICE)

January 17 is my birthday, when I celebrate the day God wanted to create me! My parents and the doctor expected me much earlier, but God scheduled the time and place I would be born (Acts 17:26). He knew my parents had just the right genes to make me, me. A part of God's character goes into the creation of every person—including me. He thought about and planned for me. He values me and has had a purpose in mind right from the beginning.

When my children were small, they listened to a lot of music, especially while riding long distances in the backseat of our car. We always played Christian music, and one song that comes to mind was written by Bill and Gloria Gaither. It says that God made you something special, "… you're the only one of your kind…."[14]

God didn't just prepare for your birth and then leave you alone to make the best of life. This is what He says in Isaiah:

> *Listen, you who count yourselves among Jacob's descendants, all the remnant of Israel. It is you, not I, who have been carried from before you were born. Indeed, when you were still in the womb, I was taking care of you. And when you are old, I will still be there, carrying you. When your limbs grow tired, your eyes are weak, And your hair a silvery gray, I will carry you as I always have. I will carry you and save you.* (Isaiah 46:3–4, VOICE)

Although those words were spoken to the children of Israel, they're just as true for His children today. It's a perfect gift He promises not just on birthdays but every day of our lives.

Thank You, Father, for making me, me!

Call in the Inspector

In my search to find out who I was, I wrote some questions in my journal. I called it "Honest to God."

- *Who am I as a person?* A daughter? Sister? Mother? Ex-wife? Friend? Employee?
- *What kind of a person am I?* Physically? Mentally? Spiritually? Emotionally? What are my talents, temperament, abilities, prejudices? What am I like at home, at work, at church?
- *What kind of a Christian am I?* In prayer? Bible study? When tempted? What fruit of the Spirit do others see in me? What is my relationship with God? What sin is there in my life? What hymns mean a lot to me, and why? How do I approach worship?
- *What 'baggage' am I carrying from the past?*
- *What kind of an impact or impression do I make on others?*
- *What are my convictions?* Are they Bible-based?
- *What do I want to do with the rest of my life?* What is God's will for me? Where will I serve Him? What are the desires of my heart?
- *How do I get from where I am to where God wants me to be?*

In the years since that journal entry, I've been working on the answers. In some areas, I believe God was happy with what He found; in others, not so much. I needed to see how God wanted me to make changes.

My life had been fifty-one years in the making, and I knew it wasn't going to change overnight. For me, this was the beginning of a long pursuit!

Are you ready for inspection?

Father, Your Word makes it clear that You will restore those who want to make a new start. Test my heart, and help me to be honest with You and with myself. Amen (1 Chronicles 29:17).

READING:
Psalm 139

Explore me, O God, and know the real me. Dig deeply and discover who I am. Put me to the test and watch how I handle the strain. Examine me to see if there is an evil bone in me, and guide me down Your path forever.
(Psalm 139:23–24, VOICE)

MID-TERMS

READING:
Deuteronomy
8:1–16

Any temptation you face will be nothing new. But God is faithful, and He will not let you be tempted beyond what you can handle. But He always provides a way of escape so that you will be able to endure and keep moving forward.
(1 Corinthians 10:13, VOICE)

I felt sick that day in high school. When I arrived for class, I found out I had crammed the wrong subject the night before and faced an exam I was unprepared to write! Thankfully God answered my prayers, brought things to my remembrance, and I managed to pass!

Do you ever wonder about the tests of life? Did you know the word test(s) occurs about 250 times in the Bible? One example is in Judges 7, where we see God cutting down Gideon's army to only three hundred men, saying He would use this small number to conquer the Midianites.

In 1 Kings 17:7–24, we read about the Zarephath widow who had lost all hope being asked to use her last bit of flour and oil to give to someone else. God allowed testing to reveal His power at work.

However, not all testing comes from God. For example, Jesus was tested by Satan and passed by remembering God's Word. Job and Joseph were also tested by the enemy's attacks, which God allowed. Satan is out to destroy our families and us, yet God still allows attacks to happen.

So, why does God test us or allow us to be tested? As mentioned above, to show us His power at work. Deuteronomy 8:2 gives us another reason. God led the Israelites through the desert for forty years so they would humble themselves and assess what was in their hearts and minds. It's not that God didn't know; He wanted them to know too!

Trials and testing can be good for us.

Help me trust You more so I can say with Job that I came forth as gold through Your testing. So may I, too, follow Your leading without turning aside. Amen (Job 23:11).

FINISHED

One of my tasks at work was being the project coordinator for various print materials. For example, one annual project required several months of work from start to finish, a two-hundred-page book that reported what was happening in the organization and how people could pray for our workers. We began by preparing database files and running reports, contacting each department for their input, finding appropriate graphics, and ensuring everything needed was included. Then, we had to edit the material to fit the allotted space.

When the graphic designer was finished, it was returned to me for proofreading. Once approved, it went to a printing company, and I needed to inspect the digital proof thoroughly. Finally, once everything was satisfactory, it was printed, and the books were delivered. I often wondered if I'd ever get through it, but once the end product arrived, there was a feeling of accomplishment.

On the cross, Jesus cried out, "It is finished." "Finished" comes from the Greek word *tetelestai*. It's a victor's shout, the cry of a person who has completed a difficult task—who has struggled through and won.

In John 17:4, we see that Jesus brought glory on earth by fulfilling everything His Father gave Him to do. Thus, the purpose for which Jesus came was accomplished. He had healed the sick, raised the dead and shown people a better way to live. In addition, He taught the disciples how to keep the faith after His own life on earth was finished. And last, but certainly not least, His death provided the way for our salvation.

None of this came easily; it caused physical and emotional pain; it brought disappointments and rejection along the way. But it was all worth it, and now, at last, it was finished.

Are there times you feel you can't keep going? Jesus 'hung in there' for you, and He asks you to do the same for Him.

Father, help me fight the good fight, finish the race set before me, and keep the faith. Amen.

READING:
John 19:28–30

I have fought the good fight, I have stayed on course and finished the race, and through it all, I have kept believing.
(2 Timothy 4:7, VOICE)

OVERDOSED ON CALORIES

READING:
1 Samuel 3:11–13;
4:12–18

Why spend money on what is not bread, and your labour on what does not satisfy? Listen, listen to me, and eat what is good...
(Isaiah 55:2, NIVUK)

Often our faith seems strongest when we sit before a greasy hamburger and fries with a large can of pop and pray, "Bless this food to do us good…!"

Looking through some old photos, I was amazed at how much thinner and healthier I was before the divorce. But then, over fifty additional pounds (22.7 kilograms) had found their way under my skin and weren't keeping themselves well hidden! 'Comfort food' was to blame for much of the weight gain. If I was alone, especially watching TV, I ate. If I was under stress, I ate. If I saw chocolate, I ate. As a result, I tired more easily, my health declined, and my clothes seemed to shrink! I had to lose weight—which is much easier said than done!

The priest Eli had two sons assisting him in the ministry. But they seduced women and made compromises in worship. For example, priests were allowed to use hooks to pull out boiled meat for their families during the sacrifice, but it seems Hophni and Phinehas hated boiled meat. Instead, they preferred the prime cuts. So when worshippers sacrificed at the temple, these two sons cut out the fillets for themselves. This addiction took its toll, with even Eli putting on too much weight (1 Samuel 4:18).

God says He doesn't give those cravings. Read 1 John 2:16 and write where they come from:_____

Psalm 78 tells us that the Israelites tested God in the wilderness by demanding the food they craved. They even spoke against Him, questioning His ability to provide. When given what they asked for, they gorged themselves; many of the sturdiest died because of their sin.

Solomon warns us that drinking too much alcohol or overeating will break us financially, cause us to sleep too much, and we'll end up clothed in rags (Proverbs 23:21). Likewise, 1 Thessalonians 5:23 reminds us to keep our bodies blameless.

Now that's something to chew on!

Father, may what I choose to eat and drink honour and glorify You (1 Corinthians 10:31). *Amen.*

BUILDING UP THE TEMPLE

Crises most definitely affect a person's health. Not only had I gained weight, but my sleep patterns went from no sleep to sleeping ten hours or more. Aches and pains crept into joints and muscles I didn't even know existed!

Setting some reasonable health goals is essential in rebuilding your life. It's good to start with a complete physical examination to identify any specific problem areas. Then, learning to eat well and possibly adding vitamins to your diet is important. Getting proper exercise should become part of your daily routine (I still need to remind myself of that!). This may mean dieting and/or joining a fitness club, sports team, riding a bike, swimming, walking or jogging.

Setting up a bedtime routine also helps in getting enough sleep, including going to bed at a regular time, having a hot beverage or a hot bath, turning off all screens, and perhaps reading instead. Ask God to take away your worries and to control your thoughts. As well, invest in a good mattress and pillow.

You need to look after yourself, especially if you have children to care for. If you've ever been on an airplane, they tell you to put the oxygen mask on yourself first and then your children. You're not much good to your family (or employer) when you drag yourself through each day.

Taking responsibility for your physical well-being brings honour to God. Are you 'fit' for the challenge?

Father, I want to honour You. Give me that shove in the right direction in not only laying out a health plan but in following it. Amen.

READING:
Psalm 139:13–18

Do you not know that your bodies are temples of the Holy Spirit, who is in you, whom you have received from God? You are not your own; you were bought at a price. Therefore honour God with your bodies.
(1 Corinthians 6:19–20, NIVUK)

HIGH CHOLESTEROL CHRISTIANS

READING:
Hebrews 12:1–3

...let us drop every extra weight, every sin that clings to us and slackens our pace, and let us run with endurance the long race set before us.
(Hebrews 12:1, VOICE)

During a medical check-up, the doctor surprised me with the news: "You have high cholesterol!" She explained there are no symptoms, but fat can build up in the blood vessels, and the blood cannot flow throughout your body as it should. Without a check-up, I wouldn't have known this was a problem until I had a stroke or heart attack.

My lifestyle had to change! I had to be more careful and watch my food intake, exercise, and lose weight.

While contemplating my physical state, I thought about how this condition could happen spiritually. Perhaps some of us are 'high cholesterol Christians!' It could be that our spiritual condition hinders the 'life-giving blood' of Christ from flowing through us.

Perhaps we need to go to the Great Physician and have a check-up. It may be that we need to watch what kind of food we're filling our minds with—from the TV, magazines, music, Internet, and questionable jokes.

We need to exercise our faith and 'run with patience the race that is set before us.' We may have to "throw off everything that hinders." For me, like most people, it's not easy to lose weight. It comes off a little at a time and sneaks back on again.

There are other 'weights' that we carry. As God reveals them to us, He will help us get rid of them—the burdens and anxious fears He doesn't expect us to bear. An old hymn by Joseph Scriven says, "Are we weak and heavy-laden, Cumbered with a load of care? Precious Savior, still our refuge, Take it to the Lord in prayer...."[15]

And, if we do these things, we'll find the love and power of Christ flowing through us once again.

Father, You have promised to give strength to the weary and increase the power of the weak (Isaiah 40:28–29). So please help me as I work on my 'weight' today. Amen.

In-Psalm-nia

It's after midnight, and you don't want to go to bed yet. But you have to work in the morning, so you crawl into bed and try, once again, to get some sleep. The thoughts come as if fired from a machine gun: *"what if...?" "if only...?" "will I ever...?" "how can I...?"* and on and on it goes. You start remembering happier times; you feel lonely. You watch the clock, and the thoughts continue. The hands of the clock seem to move either way too fast or way too slow, so you decide to read a book or watch TV—anything to remain sane until you finally drift off in the wee hours of the morning.

Do you ever have nights like that? I have!

The Psalmist David did as well, writing, *"I am worn out from my groaning; all night long I flood my bed with weeping and drench my couch with tears"* (Psalm 6:6). He also wrote, *"You have taken account of my wanderings; Put my tears in Your bottle. Are they not recorded in Your book?"* (Psalm 56:8, AMP). David also penned our verse for today.

What made the difference between sleepless, soggy nights and peaceful nights of sleep? I think it's because David came to realize that our Heavenly Father who watches over us never sleeps (Psalm 121:4). The Lord was his guardian he could rely on and talk to at any time. We also see in Psalm 55 that instead of trying to run away from his problems, David learned to turn them over to the Lord. And when he did that, he got the help he needed (vs. 6, 16–17, 22). The following verse also came from his pen, *"I lie down and sleep, I wake again, because the Lord sustains me"* (Psalm 3:5).

David was honest before God. He remembered how the Lord helped him in the past, and when he relied on that trust, he slept like a baby. Conversely, when he didn't trust the Lord, he was cowering, fearful, and unable to sleep.

How have you been sleeping lately?

Dear God, I know that you love me so much. Help me claim Your promise that when I lie down, I will not be afraid; my sleep will be sweet because I trust You. Amen (Proverbs 3:24).

Reading: Psalm 121

Tonight I will sleep securely on a bed of peace because I trust You, You alone, O Eternal One, will keep me safe. (Psalm 4:8, VOICE)

KNOCKED CENTS-LESS

READING:
Nehemiah 5

He took the five loaves and two fish, lifted his face to heaven in prayer, blessed, broke, and gave the bread to the disciples. The disciples then gave the food to the congregation. They all ate their fill. They gathered twelve baskets of leftovers. About five thousand were fed.
(Matthew 14:19–21, MSG)

After a couple of months of working and with a small bit of severance money, I was finally able to pay the first and last month's rent on a townhouse. Unfortunately, I didn't make enough, so my daughter had to co-sign the lease. Next, I had to arrange to have the electricity turned on. Since I hadn't paid the household bills in the past, I had to ask around for the electric company's name to contact them. While I was pretty good at handling finances, I knew little about household expenses. Also, with retirement not many years away, I had to prepare financially for that. I needed help!

The COVID pandemic has impacted people globally with unemployment and debt. Losing your career, especially in your later years, can cause a significant blow to your financial planning. In addition, many struggle financially for years after a divorce because divorce is costly, especially if contested.

But God has promised to supply all our needs, and He has told us not to worry. He also expects us to be prudent with money. If you've never been responsible for your finances and don't know how to rebuild them, you may need help. For a few months, make a list of everything you spend to see where your money is going and where you may be able to cut back. Check with your bank, church, or someone you know who deals with finances. See what resources, scholarships, grants, or other financial assistance may be available. Just as the people of Israel could again buy fields following their captivity, so you will be able to make strides financially—but it will take hard work, good advice, and trust in God.

It just seems to make good "cents!"

Father, thank You for meeting my needs today and for help in my financial planning. Amen.

MIRACLE OF MUSHROOMS

In the early 1930s, Mom was expecting my oldest sister. Food was scarce, costs were high, and Mom was often sick from lack of nutrition. One day a friend asked Mom to paint some silk cushions as gifts. While Mom was on her way to this lady's house to deliver them, she came across a block of land covered with mushrooms. Mushrooms had never grown there before. Delighted, she picked a basketful each day, and Dad peddled them after work. This miracle supplied their needs until Dad received his pay. That's when the mushrooms disappeared, never to grow there again.

When I was young, Mom often told stories of life during the Depression years. Those stories built up my faith that God would supply my needs. He had often met needs when my husband and I pastored small churches that couldn't always pay our total salary.

Here I was again, greatly in need. God was always faithful and often came through by the kindness of others. Utility costs were high, especially heating in the winter, but just when it was needed, I would be given an unsolicited envelope containing money. When my older daughter got married, I didn't have the money to buy a suitable dress. A few days before the wedding, someone knocked on my door and dropped off a gift of cash. It not only paid for my dress, but I could get my hair done as well!

Again and again, God supplied our every need in miraculous ways!

God is equally capable of meeting your needs as well. Where do you need a miracle?

Lord, You take such good care of birds, plants, and animals, and I know You watch over me. Thank You that You love me and take care of my every need. Amen!

READING:
Matthew 6:25–34

Look at the grass growing over there. One day it's thriving in the fields. The next day it's being used as fuel. If God takes such good care of such transient things, how much more you can depend on God to care for you, weak in faith as you are.
(Luke 12:28, VOICE)

WORRIES AND WARPED THINKING

READING:
Psalm 43

But be on guard, so that your hearts are not weighed down and depressed with the giddiness of debauchery and the nausea of self-indulgence and the worldly worries of life...
(Luke 21:34, AMP)

I left my van with the mechanic, hoping it would just need brake fluid. However, it would be about an hour before he could look at it, and the sky was getting dark. I took my new umbrella and walked towards the mall. Unfortunately, the rain started, and when I turned to cross the street, the wind took my umbrella, breaking the ribs, rendering it useless.

I wandered around the mall for a while, then phoned the mechanic. He gave me the bad news; I needed new brakes. Yes, I could put them on my credit card, but I had no money to pay that bill. Nevertheless, I gave him the go-ahead because I needed the van for work.

As I started walking back to the repair shop, it began to pour. Drenched and anxious about the repair bill, I was glad no one could tell tears were running down my face along with the rain. As I trudged across an overpass, my eyes drifted towards the swiftly moving highway traffic below. Suddenly a voice said, *"You could end it all now."* The thought frightened me, knowing it wasn't from God, yet sounding so tempting. I quickly picked up my pace and kept going.

Whenever I'm on that overpass, I think of that incident, which still gives me shivers. If I had listened to that voice, I would have missed the good things that have happened in my life since then.

After a loss, depression happens to everyone to some degree. However, trusting God, learning stress management, listening to relaxing music, or diverting our attention to something else can help us control and change our thoughts.

If you find yourself in a depressed state, talk to someone who understands. If depression has been part of your story for a prolonged period, please speak to a trained professional.

I would be in despair if I did not believe I would see Your goodness. Thank You, Father, for the hope I have in You. Amen (Psalm 27:13).

CAR TROUBLES ON MY MIND

My brother-in-law was selling a car; we worked out a payment plan so I could finally have a reliable vehicle!

I had only driven the car for a day or so when I went out one evening and noticed an interior light had come on while backing out of the driveway. I tried to switch it off, to no avail. Being in a hurry, I drove to the church with this light flickering off and on.

In my frustration, I hoped and prayed it was just a loose connection that wouldn't cost much to fix. As I parked at the church, I prayed that the car's battery wouldn't run down. Throughout our meeting, the car was constantly on my mind.

Fortunately, the car started. Driving home, I noticed that the light seemed to flicker on and off as I passed streetlights. Finally, I looked up and saw the car's uncovered sunroof. The "car trouble" was the streetlights shining through the roof!

I learned a lot from this incident, like how the devil loves to play with our minds. What we think about affects our lives and can, in turn, affect how we relate to others. We have a choice in what we think about, and God has given us a Spirit of power, love, a sound mind, and self-control. We have the option to let the devil get into our heads, or we can turn our thoughts and imaginings over to God. Our Heavenly Father wants us to have untroubled minds and to live in a state of well-being.

What do you think of that? The choice is yours.

Heavenly Father, I am at war for the battle of my mind. Help me always to choose to turn my thoughts towards the truth of Your Word. Amen.

READING:
1 Corinthians 2

Do not allow this world to mold you in its own image. Instead, be transformed from the inside out by renewing your mind. As a result, you will be able to discern what God wills and whatever God finds good, pleasing, and complete.
(Romans 12:2, VOICE)

FEELING LIKE A FAILURE

READING:
Matthew 17:14–23

... Even though our inner thoughts may condemn us with storms of guilt and constant reminders of our failures, we can know in our hearts that in His presence God Himself is greater than any accusation. He knows all things.
(1 John 3:19–20, VOICE)

When my marriage fell apart and I had to give up my career, I felt like a failure. Then, it began affecting other parts of my life until I felt like a failure at everything. Fear built up around me, and I was afraid to try new things. I didn't want to fail again.

Remembering my high school years helped. One semester I failed an exam for the first time. I was devastated! I had missed a lot of school due to illness and needed additional help in that subject. After learning what I was doing wrong, spending extra time studying, and listening more carefully to the teacher, my marks came up the next term.

Failing one exam didn't make *me* a failure. I came to learn that a failed marriage didn't mean that I was a failure either.

In today's story, the disciples had failed. What did they do about it? They asked the Lord to show them what they had done wrong and how to correct it. Perhaps the worst kind of failure is not learning anything from it.

Recovery from failure also requires forgiveness. Being human, we disappoint others, and we fail God. Healing begins with forgiveness. When we let God down, we ask forgiveness, and He forgives. When we fail others, we ask for forgiveness, and in most cases, the relationship is restored. When we mess up, we also have to forgive ourselves—realizing we're not perfect, but we are worthy of forgiveness too.

The Bible gives us story after story of people who failed. For example, look at the list of faithful people in Hebrews 11. We find a cheater, liar, murderer, prostitute, and adulterer, to name a few. But they sought forgiveness, learned from their mistakes, and placed their trust in God.

You can too!

You are gracious—it is You who makes things right. You take the side of the helpless. When we're at the end of our rope, You save us. Thank You (Psalm 116:6).

WHEREVER YOU GO

For three-and-a-half months, I looked for a job. With minimal self-esteem and the necessity of work, I felt desperate and unqualified as I looked through the employment ads.

It was a real struggle to promote myself as the best candidate for the job. I wish I could have taken my family and friends with me to cheer me on during an interview, to speak up for me when I couldn't find the right words to say. But sitting across from the person interviewing me, I was alone and unsure of myself.

Joshua was starting a new job—a big one he didn't think he could handle. Wouldn't you feel some trepidation if you had to take over from Moses?

God must have seen the terror on Joshua's face as He told him he was the new commander-in-chief. It's easy to understand why he might be afraid. Israel was untrained in warfare, and they were entering a land filled with fierce tribes who weren't going to give up without a fight. God told Joshua three times to be strong and courageous in these few verses.

But along with these exhortations, God also told Joshua why he *could* be strong and courageous. First, God had already promised them the land. Second, just as He was with Moses, He would be with Joshua. God wouldn't leave him. Third, if Joshua obeyed the Word of God, just like Moses had done, he would be successful. The bottom line was—did Joshua trust God, and was he going to obey Him?

Do you feel anxious or afraid today? God promises to be with you and give you guidance in His Word, the Bible. The bottom line is, do you trust Him?

Father, You promised to be with me wherever I go. Help me to remember You are here beside me when I feel like I can't handle what I've been asked to do. Amen.

READING:
Joshua 1:1–9

...Be strong and courageous! Do not be terrified or dismayed (intimidated), for the Lord your God is with you wherever you go.
(Joshua 1:9, AMP)

WHAT WAS I THINKING?

READING:
Isaiah 55:6–13

As the heavens are higher than the earth, so are my ways higher than your ways and my thoughts than your thoughts.
(Isaiah 55:9)

It was my first time on a plane. Shortly before Christmas, I travelled with my sister, her husband, and their toddler—as we took off, my niece and I looked out the window.

"Look, we're flying like the birdies," I said to her.

The passengers around us chuckled as she repeatedly sang, "We're flying like the birdies!" while flapping her chubby little arms. I sat back and relaxed, taking off my winter boots for more comfort.

Suddenly we hit strong turbulence. The captain told us, as if we didn't already know, adding that we were to fold our trays, lift our seatbacks into the upward position, and fasten our seatbelts. I immediately obeyed his directive and then put on my boots, thinking that if we were to crash, I didn't want to have to walk barefoot through the snow!

You're probably asking, *What was she thinking?* I know. I've asked myself that question many times. But we usually don't know how to react when we first hear scary news: "We found a lump…," "You've been served…," "I'm sorry to inform you there's been an accident…," "I've found someone else…."

What you're going through is no surprise to God, and He's prepared to get you through it. You don't always have to be strong, confident, or self-sufficient because His grace is sufficient for you and His power is made perfect in weakness (2 Corinthians 12:9).

When fears come to mind, you can repeat a favourite Bible verse over and over. Here's one, for example, *"So do not fear, for I am with you; do not be dismayed, for I am your God. I will strengthen you and help you; I will uphold you with my righteous right hand"* (Isaiah 41:10).

> *Father, You know my heart as well as my anxiety. You know the real me. Point out anything that makes You unhappy. Lead me in the way You want me to go. Amen* (Psalm 139:23–24).

A Boy and His Dad

While driving to church a few years ago, I was thinking about the many things I was dealing with at the time. I was scheduled for a biopsy the next day. I was purchasing my first home. There was my upcoming move and trying to get packing done with bursitis and tendonitis in my right arm. I thought about the long commute to work I'd have for a year, driving right across Toronto from east to west. There was also the exorbitant cost of the toll highway and the severe winter forecast. Then there was the nineteen-page legal document I had to respond to within the next two weeks. I thought about all the changes at work and the number of projects I had on the go. I was exhausted and felt like I needed to retire sooner rather than later.

In the midst of this train of thought, I drove way past the street I should have turned on to go to church. By the time I realized it, it was too late.

I carefully made my way back home and walked to the nearby park. I sat on a bench, praying that God would give me the strength to deal with everything on my plate. Then I heard voices behind me.

Two fathers and their young children had come to the park. One father suggested to his son that he run around the nearby school's racetrack. The boy began running, but he stopped after a short way, turned around, and started walking back. His father had been watching, and when he saw his son turn around, he ran to meet him. The dad took his son's hand, and together, they ran around the entire lap. And I sat on the bench with tears in my eyes.

They high-fived each other, took a rest, got up, and ran around the track again!

Thank You, Father, for this visual reminder that I can't do this alone. I need You to hold my hand and run along beside me, just as that dad did with his young boy. Amen.

READING:
Psalm 37:1–7

If you are right with God, He strengthens you for the journey; the Eternal will be pleased with your life. And even though you trip up, you will not fall on your face because He holds you by the hand.
(Psalm 37:23–24, VOICE)

THE PERFECT STORM

READING:
Mark 4:35–41

*He got up,
rebuked the wind
and said to the
waves, "Quiet!
Be still!" Then
the wind died
down and it was
completely calm.*
(Mark 4:39)

I had recently completed my contract work and was now learning to live on my small pension and meagre savings. Unfortunately, I had already lost some of those savings due to Covid-19, and we were well into the second wave. In addition, my investments were quickly sliding downhill.

Amid that upheaval, I had to replace my HVAC unit. Living in a small, older condo meant the new unit required custom fitting, and the wiring had to be upgraded to accommodate the new furnace. This meant drilling holes into my home's cement walls, which needed to be patched over once the job was done. All of this came at a hefty price.

At the same time, I negotiated a contract to publish this book. The funds weren't there yet. I felt like I was in the perfect storm. Everything seemed to be crashing down, and my white knuckles gripped the rails of the boat to keep from drowning. Where was Jesus? Why wasn't He helping me accomplish what He asked me to do?

Recalling the story from today's reading, I pictured these experienced fishermen trying to bail water, afraid in the storm. I imagined it was coming in fast and furious. I saw them trying to tighten the ropes, to keep the sails from swinging, to see their way as yet another wave broke over the boat. They couldn't see past the wall of water in front of them. They also seemed annoyed that Jesus was sleeping instead of helping them.

I was reminded that I wasn't facing my storm alone. Jesus, Himself, was in the boat with me. So, as I laid on my pillow in those wee morning hours, I took my hands off the rails of the ship and placed them in the hands of Jesus. Like the disciples, I am in awe of the One who is with us in our storms of life, the One who says, "Peace, be still!" and everything calms down.

Jesus, sometimes I just need to hang on to You for dear life. I trust You to not only calm my storms but to calm me too. Amen.

A Mountaintop Experience

Several years ago, my sister and I went up Grouse Mountain in North Vancouver, BC. From the bottom, it looked like an enormous craggy piece of rock that no one would be able to climb. Fortunately, we didn't have to climb it; we took the tram car about halfway up the mountain.

We reached a plateau you couldn't see from the bottom—flat land with all kinds of animals, buildings, and enough room for hundreds of people to walk around. We enjoyed the lumberjack show and saw a demonstration about hawks and the Peregrine Falcon, said to be the world's fastest animal. And the view was amazing!

For those braver than I, there was a ski lift to take you up even higher. In addition, a zip-line experience was advertised for those who wanted an "adrenaline-pumping tour" over the canyons way below. You could also go farther up onto the Grouse Mountain Super Skyride rooftop, sit in the café, and watch the bears.

My sister teases me because, years before, she had taken our mother up Grouse Mountain when Mom was in her eighties. When they reached the plateau, Mom saw that she could go higher and took the ski lift. At that level, she saw people paragliding, soaring through the air like eagles. Mom thought it looked fun and thought about giving it a try. But, when she asked, my sister quickly said she didn't know where to find the paragliders, and it was getting late!

Often our troubles seem like mountainous obstacles looming ahead of us. From the bottom, we see scary heights and wouldn't know there was so much life at the top. But once we allow God to carry us there, we find ourselves on a higher plain than we could have ever imagined.

Thank you, God; You have the power to lift me to higher heights than I have ever known. So help me trust You and not to be afraid. Amen.

READING:
2 Samuel 22:29–34

He makes my feet like the doe's feet [firm and swift]; He sets me [secure and confident] on my high places....
(2 Samuel 22:34 AMP)

WHO SAYS YOU CAN'T DO IT?

READING:
1 Samuel 17:1–50

Saul replied, "You are not able to go out against this Philistine and fight him; you are only a young man, and he has been a warrior from his youth."
(1 Samuel 17:33)

Times were tough—so tough that the strongest in the nation were afraid to fight the enemy. Then along came David, a young shepherd boy without military experience or the strength to wear a warrior's heavy armour. Nevertheless, he saw what needed to be done and stepped up to the plate. But then he started hearing these taunting voices… *You'll never do it! Who do you think you are? You don't have what it takes!*

There are days that we feel capable and can get out there and stand up for ourselves and what is right. But then, like David, we start to hear the voices that say, "Who are you trying to kid?"

David didn't listen to his brothers, the other soldiers, or even the king. He didn't say, "Yes, they're right," and then shrink away. Instead, he listened to his heart. David remembered God helping him in the past and was ready to step out again in faith to fight for goodness. Instead of looking at his limitations, he looked at God's power.

We can all take a lesson from the story of David and Goliath. There will be those who tell us we can never be any better than we are. There will be those, including our own inner voice, who will say, "You're not man (or woman) enough!" But by remembering God's goodness and relying on His strength, we can do the unimaginable, and others will stand in awe of God's glory in our lives.

Lord, help me remember your words to Zerubbabel, that it is not through my might or power, but through Your Holy Spirit that I will be victorious (Zechariah 4:6). Help me not to rely on my own strength but on Yours. Amen.

You've Come a Long Way!

Several months after my husband and I separated, my daughters and I lived in a rental townhouse. We didn't have much but were gradually getting a few pieces of used furniture, appliances, and dishes from here and there, and our new home was finally starting to come together. Since my mother had recently moved into a seniors' residence, my brother loaded up a truck and travelled from Manitoba to Toronto to bring me her dining room furniture.

Before this, I had been missing my wedding rings and felt a twinge of jealousy when I saw others wearing theirs. My brother had just been married, and this was the first time I met his new bride. I was amazed that I could hold her hand, look at her rings, and rejoice with her.

After my brother and sister-in-law left, I unpacked my dishes and displayed them in the dining room cabinet. I sat at the table and thought, *Gladys, you've come a long way!* I knew I still had a long way to go, but God had brought me this far, and I was able to rejoice in that.

Sometimes in our journey of healing, we're like the people in the wilderness from today's reading. Israel had come through a trying experience, yet they needed to be reminded of how far they'd already journeyed and that if they just remained faithful, God would lead them the rest of the way to the Promised Land.

Don't be discouraged. Instead, look back and see what God has already done for you. He didn't bring you this far to stop leading you the rest of the way. Continue to trust Him!

Father, thank You for what You've already brought me through. Help me to trust You to continue leading me. Amen.

READING:
Psalm 105:37–45

May the Eternal God, the God of Israel, be blessed, for He alone works miracles and wonders!
(Psalm 72:18, VOICE)

FREE FROM PAIN

Thanks to his mom, everyone thought Jabez was a pain; she called him Jabez because she 'gave birth to him in pain.' Seriously, what mother doesn't? Yet, he didn't let that stand in his way of being an honourable person or of asking God to keep him free from the pain of his past. And God granted his request, setting him free from the label someone else stuck on him!

As you look back at your past, perhaps you can still hear a parent, sibling, school bully, spouse, or someone else who labelled you. Maybe you've been called lazy, stupid, or other names so many times you've begun to believe it yourself. Have you ever said something like, "Why was I so stupid?"

Ecclesiastes 3:6 says there is a time to hold on and another to let go. Of course, we want to hang on to pleasant memories, but sometimes it's hard to let go of painful ones.

In remembering our past, our brains remind us of our emotions at that time—pleasant or not. Often our strongest memories are those that caused the strongest emotions.

God gave us the freedom to choose where to focus our thoughts. When negative memories creep into our minds, it's up to us if we decide to dwell on them or not. We can choose not to replay our past repeatedly in our minds. We can ask God to help turn our minds to other things. The choice is ours to make.

Like Jabez, you may be suffering the adverse effects of someone else's decision. But remember, he didn't let that stop him. He trusted God, who was with him through his trials, and God brought him honour and blessing.

O Father, take away the pain others have caused me and let me be free of it forever! Amen.

READING:
Romans 8:22–28

Jabez was more honorable than his brothers. His mother had named him Jabez, saying, "I gave birth to him in pain." Jabez cried out to the God of Israel, "Oh, that you would bless me and enlarge my territory! Let your hand be with me, and keep me from harm so that I will be free from pain." And God granted his request.
(1 Chronicles 4:9–10)

Saying Goodbye

I moved many times during my career. As I left each jobsite, there was always a "farewell" to close that chapter of life. Yes, I still had great memories and kept in touch with friends, but there was always that sense of finishing that stage and moving on to a new chapter.

However, when my career ended after my husband's resignation, I didn't have a chance to say goodbye to anyone. I was given notice that I couldn't serve in my ministry and was told to clean out my office. Trembling, with a tightness in my chest and too ashamed to see anyone, I snuck into the building after everyone had left to retrieve my personal belongings. It was like walking through a fog when I left the building. The pain was unbearable!

Life looked quite different with my new job and home, but there was no closure from that last chapter. I was enjoying my new career and felt it was a good place for me, yet I still thought it was temporary. I planned to return to my old job again after the required two years were up.

When I could finally apply to go back, I learned I needed to start fresh. After taking several tests and filling in many papers, I was told they would not be in a position to hire for quite some time, except for specialized positions for which I didn't qualify.

It took a long time for me to be able to say goodbye to that chapter, but it needed to be done before I could really move on.

In today's reading, we learned about people who had to move out last year's harvest to make room for the new. There comes a time when you have to say goodbye to what was, including your dreams, and accept the new life God has given you.

Lord, I'm facing a new way of living. I want my life to be filled with new joys and experiences. So help me to say goodbye to the past so I can move on. Amen.

READING:
Leviticus 26:9–13

...Forgetting what is behind and straining toward what is ahead, I press on toward the goal to win the prize for which God has called me heavenward in Christ Jesus.
(Philippians 3:13–14)

TERMITES

Our old back porch needed to be torn down—termites were to blame. Those tiny creatures can do so much harm to wood that they bring down buildings you might have thought would stand the test of time.

Termites make me think of all those little things that bother us, eating away at our minds, trying to destroy us. Did you know that termites never sleep?[16] Doesn't that sound like those annoying things you can't seem to get out of your mind—the pieces of gossip you overheard, the uncalled for remarks your ex made when you picked up your child, the friend from your past that turned the other way at the grocery store—anything that keeps you awake because you brought it home with you, fed it, and tucked it into bed with you—you just can't let it go. Perhaps it's shame from something in your past that keeps eating away at you.

Another interesting thing is that some termite queens can lay 15–25 eggs per minute, or about forty thousand eggs per day. In fact, queens in the Termitidae family can produce around ten million eggs per year.[17]

Doesn't that kind of growth sound like the snowball effect of your thinking? One thing leads to another, until those thoughts begin to take over your life?

So how do we get rid of these pesky thoughts before they destroy us? Flipping through the table of contents in *Don't Sweat the Small Stuff*,[18] author Richard Carlson advises us to choose our battles, make peace with imperfection, and surrender to the fact that life isn't always fair. Will it really matter a year from now? Did we really understand the context? Do we need to cut ourselves some slack?

Is anything "eating" at you today?

Father, as Your child, You don't want me to exhaust myself in bickering and strife, but to be gentle no matter what, tolerant and without resentment (2 Timothy 2:24). So please destroy all those things that are eating away at me and give me Your peace. Amen.

READING:
Galatians 5:13–26

But if you bite and devour one another [in bickering and strife], watch out that you [along with your entire fellowship] are not consumed by one another.
(Galatians 5:15, AMP)

WEIGHED DOWN

St. Augustine is credited with saying, "Resentment is like drinking poison and waiting for the other person to die."[19] I had preached forgiveness many times and forgiven many people for many different things, so I didn't think forgiving my ex or the Christian organization would be so hard.

It's not like I wanted them to die, but I certainly thought it would be nice if they at least apologized for causing me so much pain.

I went to a women's retreat one day because a friend was the guest speaker. I didn't know what she would talk about, but I knew God wanted me there.

READING:
Romans 12:14–21

The topic was forgiveness. My friend ended her talk by saying that if we had someone we found hard to forgive, we should take one of the small stones from the centre of the table where we sat. We were to put the stone in our pocket or purse and carry it around until we could forgive that person. Then we were to throw the stone away, representing letting it all go. I picked up a stone and looked at it. It was in the shape of a heart! I thought to myself: *How appropriate! His heart seemed as hard as that stone.*

As I was leaving the retreat's venue, I turned and went back to pick up a second stone, knowing I also had to forgive the Christian organization that had let me go without even talking to me.

I carried those two stones in my purse for what seemed like eons. Not only did I feel their physical weight, but I was also being weighed down spiritually. Resentment and bitterness were building up like poison within me. I was getting closer to the time I knew I had to make a decision.

How are you bearing up under the weight?

Lord, I know I need to forgive _____. Help me to remember that when I forgive, You will forgive me and set me free from the weight of bitterness and resentment. Amen.

Let all bitterness and wrath and anger and clamor [perpetual animosity, resentment, strife, fault-finding] and slander be put away from you, along with every kind of malice [all spitefulness, verbal abuse, malevolence].
(Ephesians 4:31, AMP)

FORGIVING IS A STONE'S THROW AWAY

READING:
Matthew 6:9–15

... And when you stand praying, if you hold anything against anyone, forgive them, so that your Father in heaven may forgive you your sins.
(Mark 11:25)

One day I received an invitation to go to the closing of the Bible school I had attended years ago. I knew there would be people I hadn't seen in years—people who had done well in their work. I didn't want them to see me and know how much I was struggling through life. I knew it would be hard for me to go back to where my former husband and I met and started dating.

However, I went and looked around. As I visited the old classrooms, the library, and the dining hall, memories flooded my mind of the good times spent there. There was a lot of laughter as friends shared remembrances of happier times.

During my visit, I quietly went alone to the chapel. I sat and looked around, with so many thoughts going through my mind—sermons from guest speakers, the beautiful harmony as we sang hymns together, the prayers of dedication that ascended to God from that sanctuary. It was there, years earlier, that I dedicated myself to work with the Christian organization I was now struggling to forgive.

The tears started to come, and it was soon time to leave. As I headed out the door of the building, I felt a small stone in my pocket. As others were gathered in groups talking, I quietly took the stone out of my pocket, dropped it among the flowers, and left it all behind. That was a healing experience for me—an opportunity to dump hurt feelings along with the stone and move on.

Are you nurturing your hurt and anger, or have you let it go?

Thank You, Lord, for walking with me through my journey towards forgiving. Thank You for knowing my struggle and gently reminding me of what I must do. Amen.

SOMEWHERE IN A CORNFIELD

For a long time after forgiving the organization, I kept feeling that heart-shaped stone I continued to carry. I would sometimes hold it in my hands, look at it, and put it back. I knew I still had to forgive my ex, but I just wasn't ready. The pain ran too deep.

Then one day, while out driving, I knew the time had come. There were no lightning bolts or thunderous voices, just a feeling deep within that I needed to be free of the weight of the hurt I still carried. No, I wasn't going to throw the stone at him. Because, like the teachers of the law and the Pharisees in today's story, I wasn't without sin.

I pulled over to the side of the country road, got out of the car, took the stone from my pocket, and threw it as far as I could into a cornfield. I got back into my car and wept. God used those tears as a visual reminder that He was cleansing me from the pain I had carried for so long.

Since then, there have been many times that the devil has tried to stir up those old feelings. "Come on, now, Gladys," I would hear him say, "you don't really think throwing a little stone can make up for all the hurt he caused!" or "Now, Gladys, maybe you could forgive him for this but did you *really* forgive him for that?"

As often as Satan has whispered those kinds of things to me, I have reminded him that somewhere in a cornfield lies a stone that God used to take away my pain and soften *my* hardened heart!

Forgive me, Lord, for thinking I deserve to be forgiven, but the person who has brought me so much pain doesn't. I don't have the strength within me to pardon _____, so I come to You to help me to forgive. Amen.

READING:
John 8:1–11

…he (Jesus) said. "If you forgive someone's sins, they're gone for good. If you don't forgive sins, what are you going to do with them?"
(John 20:23, MSG)

THE PRODIGAL SON

READING:
Luke 15:11–32

Isn't it right to join in the celebration and be happy? This is your brother we're talking about. He was dead and is alive again; he was lost and is found again!
(Luke 15:32, VOICE)

In our final six months together, I saw my former husband change into someone I didn't recognize. After he left, like the prodigal son, it seemed he spent years "squandering his life in a foreign land." Although I wasn't consistent, and sometimes it was hard, I knew God wanted me to pray for him, not that he would come back to me—but that he would have a right relationship with his Heavenly Father.

After a few years, he left that environment and moved closer to his parents and siblings. God changed his life. He returned to the church he loved, married a woman of God, and participated again on the worship team. Before long, he was asked to become a lay pastor in a small church. He accepted and continues today in that role.

It can be hard to see your ex, the person who caused you so much pain, enjoying their new life. Seeing others happy for them, pictures of them on Facebook, and hearing how well they're doing isn't easy, especially if you're alone and struggling to survive. Knowing that others are watching your reactions adds to the stress.

God loves our exes too. And we can pray that God will work in their lives as He does in our own. I've seen it happen where exes get back together and continue to serve the Lord. However, much more often, that doesn't occur. Our exes go on with their lives, and we must go on with ours.

Admittedly, I was taken aback when I learned my ex had returned to ministry. But the Lord quickly reminded me of the story of the prodigal son, and, thankfully, I was able to rejoice that my ex found his way back to His Heavenly Father and the life he loved.

Which son are you most like?

Father, guard my thoughts, words, and actions when it comes to my ex. Help me not to be like the older brother in this parable. Amen.

FREE FROM INFECTION

As previously mentioned, following a car accident, my leg became full of infection and had torn open. I eventually had surgery to close the wound. However, after several weeks, the surgical repair had partially torn open, and the infection had returned.

Sometimes forgiveness feels like that. We finally get to where we can forgive another person for hurting us. We feel healed. But then we hear a song, read something on Facebook, or see something in a store that brings back the past hurt, and the infection returns.

Jesus tells us that forgiveness is not a one-time occurrence. It's a process. I don't think He meant we are to forgive precisely 490 times, but rather that we keep doing it. Every time we feel the infection of unforgiveness, we need to choose again to forgive.

Forgiveness needs to be a lifelong habit. Ask the Holy Spirit to help you reject the thoughts that cause you to harbour resentment, blame, and unforgiveness.

Forgiveness doesn't necessarily mean reconciliation, which is sometimes impossible or unsafe. Reconciliation means both are willing to work hard at coming back together. If the other person isn't ready for that, you aren't a failure; God won't hold you responsible.

If we insist on holding grudges, we will soon find that the grudge has a hold on us. Just as with my injured leg, we need to be free of the infection of holding a grudge. Why allow the person who hurt you to keep on doing it by regurgitating that hurt over and over? Forgiveness is the only antibiotic that will bring about complete healing.

Lord, I forgave yesterday; please help me do it again today. Give me a heart of forgiveness again and again and again! Amen.

READING:
Matthew 18:21–35

Then Peter came to Him and asked, "Lord, how many times will my brother sin against me and I forgive him and let it go? Up to seven times?" Jesus answered him, "I say to you, not up to seven times, but seventy times seven."
(Matthew 18:21–22, AMP)

MEASURING UP TO GOD'S STANDARD

READING:
Nehemiah 8:1–10

The law of the Lord is perfect (flawless), restoring and refreshing the soul...
(Psalm 19:7, AMP)

If you were to look closely at some of the walls and doorframes in my condo, you would notice several are crooked. They make me wonder what measuring tools, if any, were used.

In Amos 7, we see that God gave His people a measuring tool to live by, and that tool was the Word of God. His Word is still the same for us today, but times and cultures have changed, and often it's difficult for us to understand unless we dig deeper into its meaning.

In today's reading, we find Nehemiah and the people had finished building the wall. The focus was now on how their spiritual lives measured up. They turned to the Word of God as a measuring tool. Most would have heard about these scrolls but likely had never seen or heard them read. Remember, these were written about one thousand years earlier, and many of the terms used would have changed meaning. In addition, these people had been in exile, living in a different culture. So, although they respected the Word of God, they didn't understand it until it was explained to them.

Ephesians 5:26 tells us that Christ loves His bride, the Church, and has cleansed His people by the washing with water through the Word, so I find it interesting that the events in today's reading happened by the Water Gate. Not only did the people read, respect, and try to understand the Word of God, they applied its teachings to their lives, being cleansed by it. As a result, repentance, renewal, and revival took place.

I'm sure the workmen in my condo know what a measuring tape and level are, but the problem was, they didn't apply them.

How do you measure up?

Lord, help me to be diligent in reading Your Word, accurately handling it as I apply it to my life (2 Timothy 2:15). Amen.

84

PAGES FROM THE PAST

For two years, we lived in an old house that needed work. The back porch was rotting and needed to be removed so a new addition could be put on.

The construction crew came and demolished the porch, finding a wasps' nest, termites, and some old newspapers that had been stuffed in the cracks. It was fascinating to read through those yellowed pages and see some of the good and bad news from years ago.

In today's reading, Nehemiah and the people are reading pages from the past—the good and the bad. There were lots of good things God had done for them that they had forgotten, and there were many things they wished had never taken place—things they wished they could forget.

To remember God's goodness is one of His basic commands. Almost every book of the Bible alludes to this idea. In Bible times, they used feasts and festivals to celebrate the remembrance of God's miracles. They were repeatedly reminded to remember—things like God's benefits (Psalm 103:2), how great and awesome God is (Nehemiah 4:14), the miracles He has performed (Deuteronomy 4:9), and His provision in time of need (Matthew 16:9).

Today's verse says to "commemorate"—to make a planned effort to remember God's goodness. Take time today to think about how God has led you and kept you in the past. Think about testimonies you've heard on how God has helped others. Think about your favourite Bible stories that reflect God's goodness.

> Father, help me remember the days of long ago, meditate on all Your works, and consider what You have done for me (Psalm 143:5). Amen.

READING:
Nehemiah 9:1–3, 6–25

Then Moses said to the people, "Commemorate this day, the day you came out of Egypt, out of the land of slavery, because the Lord brought you out of it with a mighty hand.
(Exodus 13:2)

THE ELEPHANT IN THE ROOM

READING:
2 Samuel 13:1–22

With the arrival of Jesus, the Messiah, that fateful dilemma is resolved. Those who enter into Christ's being-here-for-us no longer have to live under a continuous, low-lying black cloud. A new power is in operation. The Spirit of life in Christ, like a strong wind, has magnificently cleared the air, freeing you from a fated lifetime of brutal tyranny at the hands of sin and death.
(Romans 8:1 MSG)

Tamar's life changed after her half-brother Amnon raped her, and she lived as "a desperate woman" who was supposed to forget about it. But her tragedy became a giant elephant in the room; her family knew it was there, but no one knew how to get rid of it.

A staggering number of women and men have been violated sexually. Even years later, the effects haunt them and their relationships with others. Often they feel ashamed and unlovable with no value.

Some have been physically or emotionally abused, but no one wants to talk about it. Others have had an abortion or given up a baby for adoption. Those who are adopted often want to know about their birth parents but are afraid of what they might learn. Many have grown up with one parent, never knowing what the other was like or why they left. Like the elephant in the room, no one wants this awkward burden there, but they don't know how to get rid of it. And if you try to run from it, it follows you wherever you go.

There is hope for those who are carrying heavy baggage from the past. Through professional counselling and God's love and acceptance, recovery can take place. God can help sufferers identify and confess the lies they've come to believe about themselves. The Holy Spirit brings comfort from the hurts of the past. He can give a fresh start on your journey into the future (Philippians 3:13–14).

Today in your journal, identify any baggage you've been carrying and any lies you've come to believe because of it. Then write out what God says about His love and acceptance of you just as you are.

Lord, I look to You to remove my shame (Psalm 34:5). Please satisfy and refresh me like You promised and help me to forget the pain of my past (Jeremiah 31:25). Amen.

JOY RESTORED

What a joyous celebration Nehemiah and the residents of Jerusalem enjoyed. After enduring humiliation, grief, and poverty, their spiritual identity had been restored. They had listened to the Word of God and obeyed its teachings, remembering what God had done in the past and praised Him for what He would do in their future. They repented of their sins and were cleansed. They came joyfully to the celebration with thanksgiving, singing, and musical instruments.

If you've ever seen Israeli dancing, you can picture the choirs on the wall, stomping their feet, banging the tambourines, and clapping their hands. The sound of their rejoicing could be heard from far away. And I love that they put Sanballat and Tobiah in their place by proving that more than just a fox would be able to stand on the wall (Nehemiah 4:3).

Today, many people look for happiness through money and material things; some look for fame or high position; others seek fulfillment through entertainment, sex, drugs, or alcohol. If those things brought happiness, everyone in our communities would be happy. But instead, we see depression, suicide, abuse, divorce, and so on. The joy God gives doesn't come from things. God's joy comes from knowing that He loves us and cares for us.

In today's verse, Paul tells us to rejoice! And not only did he say it, but he also demonstrated it. He was a man who had faced poverty and been beaten. He had a 'thorn in the flesh,' had been in a shipwreck, and was now writing from a Roman prison. In this letter to the Philippians, he speaks about joy or rejoicing sixteen times in four chapters. He set an example for what to do even when things don't go the way we had hoped—we are to rejoice!

And why rejoice? Because God is in control.

Heavenly Father, "Let my passion for life be restored, tasting joy in every breakthrough you bring to me. Hold me close to you with a willing spirit that obeys whatever you say" (Psalm 51:12, TPT). Amen.

READING:
Nehemiah 8:9–12;
12:27, 38–43

Rejoice in the Lord always. I will say it again: Rejoice!"
(Philippians 4:4)

Jumpin' Jehoshaphat!

Going through a divorce was difficult—yet I was praising the Lord!

I had been at my new job for several months when my birthday rolled around. It was the custom for our staff to celebrate birthdays during a coffee break, and co-workers often put balloons and streamers around the desk of the person being celebrated. But on my birthday, nothing happened. I didn't say anything, but I thought it was rather odd and felt disappointed. They had forgotten my special day.

About five weeks later, the staff surprised me with a birthday party. And I mean surprised! The person in charge of birthdays realized the mistake, and now was the time to make up for it. My boss gave me a book on praise—*31 Days of Praise* by Ruth Myers—and I began reading it that day.

READING:
2 Chronicles
20:18–30

Give thanks to the Lord, for his love endures forever.
(2 Chronicles 20:21)

It turned out that God's timing was perfect. It was during those thirty-one days that my divorce became final. That book helped me to praise God throughout those emotional weeks.

In today's reading, we see that Jehoshaphat faced a difficult time. And what did he do? He praised God!

Generally, when we face a problem, we scramble to do something—write a plan, set goals, get counselling, read a book about it, seek advice, pray. Of course, these are good, but one of the most important things is to praise!

Jehoshaphat gathered his people to praise God. He even appointed a 'worship team' to lead into the battlefield. Their job was to sing and praise the Lord for His holiness.

How do you face your problems? With praise? It sure helped Jehoshaphat, and it can sure help you!

Lord, I praise You for the glorious sights I see in the sky above me and all around me. You ordained praise to silence Your enemies, and I praise You for that too! How majestic is Your name throughout the earth (Psalm 8). Amen.

WORSHIP FIT FOR THE KING

Many years ago, I was privileged to be invited to attend an interdenominational worship service at which Queen Elizabeth was present.

I watched as the Queen and her procession entered the service. I saw the red carpet, the floral arrangements, the dignitaries, and the little girl who presented a bouquet of flowers to Her Majesty.

The service was well planned. There was participation by men and women, young and old, and various nationalities, all speaking in their native language.

I listened to the various choirs sing beautiful hymns of praise and the school band that played so well. Scriptures were read, and I heard the prayers and the Bible message so well presented.

Yes, in all, it was a worship service fit for a Queen!

I may never again have the opportunity to attend a service with royalty, but I am reminded that I am in the presence of the King of kings every time I worship!

Read Psalm 100:4. How are we to come to worship?

_____

Read I Chronicles 16:29. What does this say about worship?

_____

_____

Our reading today also reminds us to have "clean hands and a pure heart."

Is your worship fit for the King?

Father, I love You, and I join the heavenly host in making a joyful noise of praise to You. You are so good, loving, and kind. Thank You for all You have done for me. Amen.

READING:
Psalm 24

... true worshipers will worship the Father in spirit [from the heart, the inner self] and in truth; for the Father seeks such people to be His worshipers.
(John 4:23, AMP)

Amazing Care

I parked my car at a different mall entrance than usual. Then, feeling turned around in the mall, I thought, *Why on earth did I park there?* Well, on the way out, I got my answer!

As I headed out the door, an older woman stopped to ask if I was heading to Sheppard Avenue. Obviously exhausted, and close to tears, she wanted to catch the bus but didn't have the energy to walk to the bus stop. I felt sorry for her, at the same time wondering if I should take a complete stranger in my car. A little voice inside me told me it would be okay.

As we neared Sheppard Avenue, I asked her which way she was going. Since she was heading my way, and there was no bus in sight, I decided to take her further. I learned the woman's name was Elaine. She was from Hamilton and had come to Toronto that day to lead a workshop and was now on her way to visit a friend. Arriving at my next turn-off, I discovered Elaine also needed the same route. As it turned out, I took her all the way to her destination—one block from where I lived! As Elaine left the car, she thanked Jesus and me. I told her I was a Christian too, and she said, "It's amazing how God looks after me!"

Yes, it was amazing. In an area with over six million people, God brought two complete strangers together at a mall entrance at just the right time, both heading to one block from each other.

Be reminded today that God takes care of His own and uses us to help others.

God, help me to remember You care more about me than I do. You know every detail about me, even the number of hairs on my head right now! (Luke 12:7). Help me to rest in Your care. Amen.

READING:
Luke 12:24–26

Think about those crows flying over there: do they plant and harvest crops? Do they own silos or barns? Look at them fly. It looks like God is taking pretty good care of them, doesn't it? Remember that you are more precious to God than birds!
(Luke 12:24, VOICE)

DOWN TO THE LAST DETAIL

My little granddaughter skinned her knee and went to her mom for a bandage. Can you imagine if my daughter had said: "Don't come to me if you have a bumped knee, a sliver, or a cut lip. Only come to me if you're hurt so bad you need to go to the hospital."

How often do we only go to our Heavenly Father with the 'big stuff' but try to handle all the little things ourselves? We figure God has bigger problems to manage and isn't interested in our minor issues.

But that's not what I see in the Bible! Instead, God shows His interest in missing teeth (Exodus 21:27) and grazing rights (Exodus 22:5–6). He cared about one lost coin, one lost sheep, and one lost son (Luke 15). Jesus cared about the refreshments at a wedding (John 2:1–11). He didn't want people to go hungry because they stayed to listen to Him (John 6:1–14). He joined two sisters weeping at the death of their brother (John 11:17–36).

Read John 19:26. Whose welfare did Jesus care about while dying on the cross?

READING:
Matthew 10:29–31

The Lord directs the steps of the godly. He delights in every detail of their lives.
(Psalm 37:23, NLT)

_____

God even knows how many hairs are on your head (Matthew 10:30). So whether you have a full head of hair, or you've lost it all because of genetics, shaving, or disease—God cares about every detail!

Do you trust God with the big things as well as the little things in your life? He cares and has the power to help.

Father, how can I ever trust You with the big things in my life if I don't trust You with the little things? Thank You for being the God of details and for caring about me. Amen.

IS GOD A TENOR?

READING:
Zephaniah 3:14–17

...and He is the champion who will rescue you. He will joyfully celebrate over you; He will rest in His love for you; He will joyfully sing because of you like a new husband.
(Zephaniah 3:17, VOICE)

When my daughters and grandchildren were babies, I often calmed them down by singing to them. As I cuddled and sang softly to them, their crying would change to whimpers, and soon they would be asleep or ready to laugh again and play.

When my daughters were a little older, I sang to them as part of their bedtime routine. After they said their prayers, we would sing a Sunday school chorus or two, then end with "Jesus Loves Me." Then, after singing through the verses, I would make up words about their day's events or what they would be doing the following day. Frequently, they ended up being quite comical as I tried to make the lines rhyme! Sometimes they would make up the words, and we would sing them together. But I was trying to teach them that, through it all, Jesus loved them no matter what their day was like.

That's the picture I see when I read today's verse. Our "Daddy" takes great delight in us, and as He tucks us in at night and even throughout the day, He rejoices over us with singing. I picture Him making up the words according to our days—words meant personally for us, words that tell us of His love.

There are many 'love songs' on the radio, TV, music apps, and YouTube, but none of them can compare to the song of love God has written just for you.

Why not take a few moments right now and listen? Do you hear Him singing?

Father, help me to rejoice in Your presence and listen to Your love song for me. Amen.

BLESS ME

"Oh" is a little word with a big punch! If we were writing this verse today, we would probably say, "OOOOOOOOH, that You would bless me!!!" In these few words, Jabez expressed his deepest desire and utter dependence upon God. He was confident the Lord would bless him. And we see at the end of verse 10, God didn't disappoint him.

We can thank David Wilkinson and David Kopp for bringing these verses to life in their book *The Prayer of Jabez*. Jabez was an honourable man and better than his brothers. But, unfortunately, that's about all we know of him, except for his deep desire to be blessed by God.

Today we don't fully understand the concept of the blessing (although there are several books to help us). But to the Israelites, it meant everything. It was so important, Esau vowed to kill his brother, Jacob, for stealing it from him (Genesis 27:30–41).

READING:
1 Chronicles
4:9–10

As I look back over the years, I see the many ways God has blessed me. One of those times was when I bought my small condo. It was a time when purchasing a home meant bidding wars, and people often ended up paying thousands over the asking price. But I didn't have the budget to participate in bidding wars. So God found me a place and set the time just right. I purchased my home slightly below the asking price. Shortly after, the cost of housing soared. I wouldn't have been able to get my own place at any other time.

Oh, that you would bless me...
(1 Chronicles 4:10)

Several years before my divorce, I thought I would like to write when I retired and help others write their God stories. I had always loved reading and had done a little writing before that. God enabled me to learn more about writing, editing, and publishing through my second vocation. He took the desires of my heart and blessed me by providing some basic training towards accomplishing my goal.

How much do you want the blessing of God in your life? If we pray this prayer out of the same longing Jabez did, He will grant our request, just like he did for Jabez. In fact, God was so impressed with this short prayer He recorded it for our benefit!

O Father, bless me! Amen.

GIVE ME MORE

When I started my last job, I felt outside of my comfort zone. Although I was still involved in ministry, it was totally different from what I had done in the past. It was scary, but God spoke to me through a cartoon in the local paper. I hung it up in my workstation for several years after as a reminder!

The cartoon was black and white with a woman struggling to get out of the box she was in. The last frame of the comic strip showed her with one foot out and the other ready to step out of the box, and in this frame, her new world was in colour.

In today's Bible verse, Jabez asked God to take him out of his comfort zone and bless him with even more work to do. In fact, he wanted it so badly, there is an exclamation point after it!

I've seen this happen in others, and it's happened in my own life as well when I have prayed this prayer. Where I once ministered to a small group of people, my new job gave me a ministry that extended across Canada and the world!

Since praying that prayer, God has blessed me with various ministries, from writing magazine articles to helping publish missionary stories in several books, writing this book, and having material on the Internet that can be seen worldwide. In addition, He has provided me with people interested in starting small groups; I've been able to organize special events and so much more. Who knows what else will come my way?! Serving God is exciting!

Today's reading tells us to enlarge our tents, open them wide, and not hold back. God has so much more to offer you. All you need to do is ask.

O Father, give me more—more of your love, peace, joy, strength, resources, and a ministry where I can share Your love with others. Amen.

READING:
Isaiah 54:2–3

Oh, that you would bless me and enlarge my territory!
(1 Chronicles 4:10)

SHOW COMPASSION

Just as God has given us each unique abilities, I believe He has, through our crises, given us a particular passion for a specific type of people. As a result, He may ask us to share our story with others one-on-one, or perhaps write our story or share our testimony in a church setting.

If you have seen your children suffer, God may give you a passion for helping other children of divorced parents. You may see other single parents within your community, and God may ask you to form a support group with them. As you heal, God may want you to share the hope that is in you through Christ Jesus.

READING:
Colossians 3:12–17

He consoles us as we endure the pain and hardship of life so that we may draw from His comfort and share it with others in their own struggles.
(2 Corinthians 1:4, VOICE)

Some people have suffered so much that they want to encourage and support others to keep them from suffering too. I think of Joni Eareckson Tada, who visits people worldwide, sharing insights into living as a quadriplegic and providing wheelchairs to many in need. She took her pain, turned it around, and used it to bring God's message of love to others. People who have lost a loved one to a drunk driver are now passionately serving in groups like Mothers Against Drunk Drivers (MADD). Books have been written, support groups formed, and stories shared by those who have suffered and want to help others going through similar circumstances.

At some point, God will give you a passion for serving Him in a way no one else can do. Others need to hear your story of hope, how God is bringing you through or has already brought you through.

God wants you to learn more about Him through your divorce, as well as any other crisis you may face. In addition, your experience can bring glory to God as you share with others what He has done and is doing in your life.

Who and what are you passionate about?

Lord, open my eyes to the needs of those around me and focus them on the people You want me to reach with Christ's love. Amen.

BLOOM WHERE YOU'RE PLANTED

I watched as the guest florist at our women's retreat showed us how to separate plants and repot them. As her hands pulled the roots of the beautiful plant apart, I shivered. It took me back to when my husband and I were torn apart. I was reminded of how much it hurt to no longer be one but to be split in two, him going one way and me another.

As the florist put the plants into new pots, I saw myself being taken out of my familiar surroundings and put into a different environment where I was expected to grow and blossom.

READING:
Philippians 1:3–14

This uprooting and replanting reminded me of our time in Halifax. A tree had been cut down in our backyard. It was too costly to remove the stump, so we built a rock garden around it.

One flower, in particular, grew, and grew, and grew! We had obviously chosen a type of plant that you wouldn't typically see in a rock garden. Being somewhat embarrassed, I hoped our neighbours wouldn't notice. I thought that flower would only last a short while, but it bloomed, and bloomed, and bloomed!

During those months the flower bloomed, I was recuperating from major surgery. I don't know how many times I looked out my kitchen window and saw that beautiful flower as it swayed in the wind, got drenched by rain, and glistened in the sun. I vowed to always bloom where I was planted.

After painful separation and being planted in a brand-new environment, God helped me to spread my roots deep and blossom, hopefully bringing as much blessing to others as that flower in my rock garden brought to me.

Have you been taken out of your comfort zone and transplanted somewhere you don't think is right for you? Like that flower and the Apostle Paul, you can grow deep roots, and God can use you right where you are.

Father, help me to see that what has happened to me can advance the Gospel. Help me to bloom where I'm planted. Amen.

Picture this: It's midnight. In the darkness of their cell, Paul and Silas—after surviving the severe beating—aren't moaning and groaning; they're praying and singing hymns to God. The prisoners in adjoining cells are wide awake, listening to them pray and sing.
(Acts 16:25, VOICE)

FOCUSING ON THE I'S

When I first realized that God wanted me to share what He had brought me through, it scared me! *Why would anyone read anything I write? Others have been through much worse; wouldn't they make better witnesses?*

In today's reading, we see that God will do the heavy work; Moses simply had to obey. But somehow, Moses got his wires crossed and thought it was up to him. Instead of focusing on God ("I have come down to rescue them"), Moses focused on himself ("Who am I, that I should go...")

Isn't that often the way with us? Who would have expected an older man, who had difficulty expressing himself, to be God's spokesperson and lead His people to the Promised Land? Who would have expected a rough fisherman like Peter to preach loving sermons or a Jew named Saul, who murdered Christians, to preach the love of Christ to the Gentiles?

Who, but God, could work through such misfits? But that's just what He does. God may lead you to do something no one else can do. There may be someone somewhere depending on you to follow through.

God may use your challenging situation to bring you to a place where you can use what you've learned to help others. But He doesn't leave you to face it alone. You can count on Him to be faithful in fulfilling His part.

When I knew God wanted me to write this book, I was terrified and kept putting it off. In my mind, I kept hearing, *Who are you to write such a book? Who cares what you have to say?*

When God calls us to do something, He also equips us. We need to obey and leave the results to Him.

Whose "I's" are you focusing on?

Lord, help me to remember You will never lead me where Your grace cannot keep me. Amen.

READING:
Exodus 3:7–15

But Moses said to God, "Who am I, that I should go to Pharaoh and bring the Israelites out of Egypt?"
(Exodus 3:11)

DIRTY FEET

Growing up in southern Manitoba, I loved to see the array of colours in the various crops in the fields. Flying over it was even better, like you were looking down at a patchwork quilt. So, it's difficult to imagine that in this fertile land lies the Spirit Sands Desert—sand dunes that shift with the wind, cacti and all.

While visiting home for a family reunion, many of us decided to hike in this small desert area. Even though I grew up nearby, I had never taken the opportunity. Unfortunately, it was a scorching, humid summer day, and I only had two pairs of shoes with me. I had to choose between bare feet in my good sandals or socks and sneakers. Not wanting to ruin my sandals or get sand between my toes, I decided on the sneakers. Big mistake!

After hiking for a while, we stopped at a spot overlooking the Devil's Punch Bowl. My feet were aching, so I took off my shoes and socks. Another big mistake! Ew—eee, did my feet stink! While the others wrinkled their noses, I quickly threw my shoes and socks into my backpack and put on my sandals.

Hiking back, I was much more comfortable. Although everyone had showered that morning, our feet were filthy by the time we finished the hike. There was a water pump near the exit, so we took off our shoes and stood in a circle to take a picture of our dirty feet before washing them.

We can be in the middle of a day where life is good, and we are growing in our Christian walk. But then, we make a choice that we regret—a choice that makes us spiritually stinky, and we need cleansing, just like we needed to clean our feet from our trek through the desert.

So, how clean are your feet today? Do you need to ask Jesus to bring the basin and towel?

Lord, as I confess my sins to You, I know I can depend on You to forgive and make me clean. Take away the stench of my wrong-doing (I John 1:9). Amen.

READING:
John 13:1–10

Jesus answered, "Those who have had a bath need only to wash their feet; their whole body is clean..."
(John 13:10)

99

ONGOING UPKEEP

With the purchase of my first home, I quickly learned that ongoing upkeep and repairs are necessary. The longer things get left in disrepair, the worse they become. The workers who rebuilt the wall around Jerusalem learned that lesson the hard way when they forgot about their commitments to God and fell back into their old ways.

The journey we've been on these past ninety days is just the beginning of a new life for you—a life that will be rebuilt, restored, and renewed. At the end of this book, you will find a list of recommended readings and other resources to add to your toolbox. From here, I hope you'll go on to dig deeper into the areas God leads you to work on.

I leave you with these words:

READING:
Philippians 1:4–11

Finally, brothers and sisters, rejoice! Strive for full restoration, encourage one another, be of one mind, live in peace. And the God of love and peace will be with you.
(2 Corinthians 13:11)

Do not allow this world to mold you in its own image. Instead, be transformed from the inside out by renewing your mind. As a result, you will be able to discern what God wills and whatever God finds good, pleasing, and complete… devote your minds to sound judgment since God has assigned to each of us a measure of faith… don't hide behind a mask; love authentically. Despise evil; pursue what is good as if your life depends on it… Do not slack in your faithfulness and hard work… Do not forget to rejoice, for hope is always just around the corner. Hold up through the hard times that are coming, and devote yourselves to prayer… If people mistreat or malign you, bless them. Always speak blessings, not curses… If it is within your power, make peace with all people… do not seek revenge… Never let evil get the best of you; instead, overpower evil with the good.
(Romans 12:2–3, 9, 11–12, 14, 18, 21, VOICE)

Father, You have begun a good work in me and will not stop in mid-design but will keep perfecting me until Jesus returns (Philippians 1:6). Amen.

ABOUT THE AUTHOR

From Sunday school, children's choir, youth group, Girl Guides, music lessons and other activities, my life growing up on the Canadian Prairies was full.

While raising my family, I served in various positions in several churches across Western Canada. This was followed by a few years in public relations, two years in a Christian bookstore, and community services. Following my divorce, I continued to serve the Lord in a lay position in the field of communications.

All my life, I have enjoyed reading, writing, and photography. Other hobbies include learning about my family's history and helping others share their life stories.

I have two daughters who live nearby with their families.

You can learn more about me and my story at www.faithbooking.ca

RESOURCES FOR YOUR TOOLBOX

Allen, Jennie. 2020. *Get Out of Your Head*. Colorado, CO: WaterBrook.

Ashleigh-Connolly, Jessica. 2019. *You Are the Girl for the Job*. Grand Rapids, MI: Zondervan.

Augustine, Sue. 2005. *When Your Past is Hurting Your Present*. Eugene, OR: Harvest House Publishers.

Bevere, John. 2011. *The Bait of Satan*. Lake Mary, FL: Charisma House.

Cloud, Henry and Townsend, John. 2001. *Boundaries with Kids*. Grand Rapids, MI: Zondervan.

Conway, Jim. 1990. *Adult Children of Legal or Emotional Divorce*. Downers Grove, IL: InterVarsity Press.

Fisher, Bruce and Alberta, Robert. 2016. *Rebuilding When Your Relationship Ends*. Oakland, CA: New Harbinger Publications, Inc.

Gaither, Gloria, 1980. *Because He Lives*. Tarrytown, NY: Fleming H. Revell Company.

Gordon, Jeenie. 1991. *Cementing the Torn Strands*. Tarrytown, NY: Fleming H. Revell Company.

Grosmaire, Kate. 2016. *Forgiving My Daughter's Killer*. Nashville, TN: Nelson Books.

Leadingham, Everett (editor). 1995. *A Christian Attitude Toward Attitudes*. Kansas City, MO: Beacon Hill Press.

Ortberg, John. 2010. *The Me I Want to Be*. Grand Rapids, MI: Zondervan.

Smoke, Jim. 1995. *Growing Through Divorce*. Eugene, OR: Harvest House Publishers.

Smoke, Jim. 2000. *Moving Forward*. Peabody, MA: Hendrickson Publishers, Inc.

Sprague, Gary. 1992. *My Parents Got a Divorce*. Colorado Springs, CO: David C. Cook Publishing.

Terkeurst, Lysa. 2018. *It's Not Supposed to Be This Way*. Nashville, TN: Thomas Nelson.

Terkeurst, Lysa. 2020. *Forgiving What You Can't Forget*. Nashville, TN: Thomas Nelson.

Thompson, Mark Ian. 2010. *Splashing Over*. Winnipeg, MB: Word Alive Press.

Toler, Stan. 2001. *The Buzzards are Circling, But God's Not Finished with Me Yet*. Colorado Springs, CO: David C. Cook.

Underwood, Ed. 2008. *When God Breaks Your Heart*. Colorado Springs, CO: David C. Cook Publishing.

Walls, David. 1977. *Ordinary Heroes*. Denver, CO: Accent Publications.

Walsh, Sheila. 2017. *In the Middle of the Mess*. Nashville, TN: Thomas Nelson.

Walsh, Sheila. 2018. *It's Okay Not to Be Okay*. Grand Rapids, MI: Baker Books.

Young, Ed. 1996. *From Bad Beginnings to Happy Endings*. Nashville, TN: Thomas Nelson.

Youssef, Michael. 2016. *God, Help Me Rebuild My Broken World*. Eugene, OR: Harvest House Publishers.

Divorce information, www.divorcenet.com.

Divorce recovery support groups, www.divorcecare.org.

Divorce videos and podcasts, www.divorcemag.com.

DivorceCare for Kids, www.DC4K.org.

Focus on the Family blogs on divorce, www.focusonthefamily.com/?s=divorce.

Organization for single parents, www.parentswithoutpartners.org.

Recovery after divorce, www.rebuilding.org.

TOPICAL INDEX

U

Understanding — 2; 11; 17; 21; 22; 39; 45; 46; 53; 55; 66; 78; 84; 93

Upkeep — 100

V

Values — 47; 56; 86

Vengeance (see Bitterness)

Victory — 20; 59; 74

W

Weakness — 29; 50; 54; 56; 62; 70

Withdrawal — 49; 50

Witness — 35; 85; 96; 98

Worry — 31; 49; 61; 62; 64; 66; 67; 69; 70; 71; 72

Writing (also see Journaling) — xiii-xiv; 1; 2; 95; 96

Scripture Index

NEW TESTAMENT

ENDNOTES

Healing Takes Time

1. Margaret Atwood Quotes. Brainy Media Inc., 2022. Accessed August 6, 2021, from
   https://www.brainyquote.com/quotes/margaret_atwood_146159

A Journey of a Thousand Miles

2. Lao Tzu, BBC World Service. Accessed September 3, 2021, from https://en.wikipedia.org/wiki/
   A_journey_of_a_thousand_miles_begins_with_a_single_step

Trust the Architect

3. Conner-Murphy, Amy, Blog October 14, 2013, Accessed September 3, 2021, from 10 Things an Architect
   Does For You | ACM Design Architecture & Interiors (acmdesignarchitects.com)

White-out Conditions

4. Moore, James W. (2010). *When the World Takes the Wind Out of Your Sails*. Abingdon Press. p. 86

You've Got the Power

5. Fact Check:
   • Northeast blackout of 2003 - Wikipedia, accessed November 2021, from https://en.wikipedia.org/wiki/
     Northeast_blackout_of_2003
   • The great North America blackout of 2003 | CBC Archives, Accessed August 2021, from https://www.cbc.
     ca/archives/the-great-north-america-blackout-of-2003-1.4683696
   • January 1998 North American ice storm - Wikipedia, accessed from https://en.wikipedia.org/wiki/
     January_1998_North_American_ice_storm#:~:text=The%20North%20American%20Ice%20
     Storm%20of%201998%20(also,York%20to%20central%20Maine%20in%20the%20United%20States
   • Ice Storm of 1998 | The Canadian Encyclopedia, accessed from https://www.thecanadianencyclopedia.
     ca/en/article/ice-storm-1998

You Raise Me Up

6. Warner, Sandy, "To Fly Like an Eagle: Facts & Parables of Mentoring." Blog accessed from
   https://www.riedelfamilyltl.com/birds/faq-how-high-can-an-eagle-soar.html

Built by Wisdom

7. The Serenity Prayer is attributed to Richard Neibuhr, Public Domain.

No Longer Disgraced

8. Depression is a very complicated matter. If you find yourself stuck in depression, please check with your
   doctor or counsellor.

Boundary Lines

9. Carder, Dave; Henslin, Earl; Townsend, John; Cloud, Henry; Brawand, Alice. (1995). *Secrets of Your Family Tree*. The Moody Bible Institute of Chicago. p 170

Fuel for Revenge

10. Reiner, Rob (Director) (1987). *The Princess Bride*. Act III Communications.
11. McMillen, S.I. (1963). *None of These Diseases*. Old Tappan, NJ: Fleming H. Revell Co. p. 68

Something Beautiful

12. Gloria Gaither, Because He Lives (Tarrytown, NY: Fleming H. Revell Company, 1980), 70
13. Gaither, Gloria. (1997). *Because He Lives*. Grand Rapids, MI: Zondervan Publishing House. p. 72

Happy Birthday

14. Gaither, William J. (1975). "I Am a Promise," *The Very Best of the Very Best for Kids*. A & M. Lyrics accessed from https://www.letssingit.com/gaither-vocal-band-lyrics-you-re-something-special-p3zzzj2

High Cholesterol Christians

15. Scriven, Joseph M. (1855). "What a Friend We Have in Jesus." Public Domain

Termites

16. "Termite Facts: 10 Things About Termites You Should Know. Accessed September 13, 2021 from https://www.resteasypestcontrol.com/termite-facts-the-truth-about-termites/
17. "20 Unbelievable Facts About Termites," Blog (May 6, 2021). Accessed September 13, 2021 from https://plunketts.net/blog/20-unbelievable-facts-termites
18. Carlson, Richard (1997). *Don't Sweat the Small Stuff*. Hachette Books

Weighed Down

19. Saint Augustine Quotes, Brainy Media Inc., 2022. Accessed September 6, 2021 from https://www.brainyquote.com/quotes/saint_augustine_384531